BOOKS FOR PLEASURE

POPULAR FICTION

1914–1945

by

Suzanne Ellery Greene

Bowling Green University Popular Press
Bowling Green, Ohio 43403

The Popular Press is the publishing division of the Center for the Study of Popular Culture, Bowling Green University, Bowling Green, Ohio, Ray B. Browne Director.

Library of Congress Catalog Number: 74-17776

ISBN: 0-87972-097-2 Paperback
ISBN: 0-87972-098-0 Clothbound

Printed in the United States of America

for

Jennifer

CONTENTS

ACKNOWLEDGMENTS

After any three and a half year long undertaking, many acknowledgments are due. I take this opportunity to thank only a few of the people who have helped and borne with me during the writing of this book.

First thanks go to my parents who always encouraged me in my endeavors.

A number of people I knew when I was an undergraduate at Harvard University proved to be of lasting inspiration. Professor Donald Fleming and Professor Giles Constable opened my mind to the joys of history. Professor David Riesman taught me much about social analysis. Dean Catherine Williston encouraged striving for excellence.

The technical problems of the book were made considerably easier by the help of Miss Adelaide Eisenhart and Mrs. Ione Hoover of the Inter-Library Loan Division of The Johns Hopkins University's Eisenhower Library. They scouted down the oldest and longest lost of the best sellers for me, often finding them in obscure parts of the country.

At Johns Hopkins, there are many people to thank. For advice, and especially encouragement, I owe much to my colleagues Harold Livesay and Patrick G. Porter. I received help from many members of the faculty, of whom three require special recognition. Professor Warren S. Torgerson of the Psychology Department gave invaluable advice on the use of statistics and methods. Professor Charles Barker of the History Department gave excellent criticism and provided many helpful suggestions. This book began as a doctoral dissertation, and to my dissertation adviser, Professor Alfred D. Chandler, Jr., I owe thanks not only for the help he gave me in this project but for his attitude of tolerance throughout my entire graduate school career.

Finally, I would like to thank the Johns Hopkins University administration for the financial support given during the course of the research and writing of this book.

CHAPTER 1

INTRODUCTION: PHILOSOPHY AND METHODS

Popular fiction has been neglected as a mode for the study of attitudes and values, yet it is a particularly appropriate means to obtain from one source a reflection of thought and beliefs in a wide range of areas. This is a study of the best selling novels that appeared in the United States from 1914 to 1945. These best sellers provide an insight into a wide range of changing American attitudes and values from the beginning of World War I to the end of World War II. A novel can touch on all phases of life. The novels reflect opinions on both social and personal concerns in a quantity comparable to general interest in those areas.

One of the working assumptions of this study is that novels do reflect the attitudes and values of the people who read them. Novels, certainly best selling novels, are read for pleasure. The reader therefore exercises a great deal of choice over which novels he will read. Certainly he is not forced to read any. It appears that most readers have some acquaintance with a novel before they read it. They can choose a novel as they would choose a friend. The most popular books are ones that the reader can understand or feel close to as he would to a friend. A book is particularly appealing if it seems to reinforce views already held by the reader. Therefore much can be learned about readers by knowing which books the greatest numbers choose to read. James D. Hart, in *The Popular Book*, comments on the representation of popular thought by best sellers:

The taste of the largest number of readers is shaped by contemporary pressures more than is the taste of the highly cultivated reader, who has a deeper background of aesthetic experience and knowledge to guide him. Books flourish when they answer a need and die when they do not. The needs of the greatest reading public are various: they include classification of ideas already in circulation; emotional statement of feelings that people are prepared to accept; popularization of desirable information heretofore obscure, satisfying appeal to forms of entertainment currently considered amusing or exciting . . . In some way or another, the popular author is always the one who expresses the people's minds and paraphrases what they consider their private feelings. This combination of social history, cultural history, and literary taste tacitly involves itself in the question, which came first, the chicken or the egg?—the popular book that shaped public interest or the public interest that shaped the book's popularity? Sometimes one can say clearly it is the first, sometimes the second; most often one can answer only in terms of a dynamic interplay of reader, writer, and the times in which both lived.[1]

Novels, of course, are not all uniform in their interests or values even in any one year. Neither, however, is society at large. Individuals rarely live without conflicting and ambivalent sets of attitudes and values. The novels, in the manner of an unannounced public opinion poll, indicate the trends. They show which values continue over a large number of years, and they indicate when newer forms of thought begin to gain popularity and then gradually replace the older. The books indicate which values are accepted with a degree of unanimity and which ones are the subject of dispute during a given time period.

If it is true that the novels reflect the readers' point of view, it must be shown that the readers do have some foreknowledge of the books they read. Many factors indicate that most readers do indeed have some idea about the contents of a book when they choose to read it rather than other books available at the time.

If a potential reader sees a book on the shelf of a bookstore, the jacket may provide the only information about the contents. A picture of a woman and two children or of a farm house points to a different kind of story from what one would expect to find in a book with a jacket picturing a woman wearing a low-cut scarlet dress. The back of the jacket may contain comments about a wholesome New England family or a passionate love affair that brought scandal to the court of a king. Some hint about the type of book is conveyed. Beyond this, booksellers usually read most of the new books that come into their stores and will describe them for the prospective reader. An official of a national chain of book stores has written that a bookseller is first interested in a book when he sees that a large group of people might become interested in it. The publisher can influence the bookseller's attitude here. Once the bookseller is convinced, his enthusiasm helps push sales upward.[2]

Often the buyer has read a review of the book. Even more likely, someone has recommended the book to the prospective buyer or has, at least, discussed it in his presence. Another possibility is that the buyer is already acquainted with other books by the same author. A best selling author acquires a following who will read all that he publishes. In the list of books used in this study, fifty-four of the total one hundred and forty-five were written by authors who have appeared earlier on the list.

Book clubs are responsible for sales of large numbers of copies of best sellers. Even these clubs which are so criticized for limiting the readers' choice allow a certain amount of selectivity. Members are not required to take a book each month. Most of the clubs offer some alternative to their primary monthly selection, neither of which the member has to buy. Furthermore, the clubs send pamphlets describing all the possible selections to accompany all order forms, thus providing another source of information about current books.

The book clubs are not necessarily creators of best sellers. Instead they provide one more source of knowledge about books rather than monopolizing the selection. The first two major book clubs in America, the Book-of-the-Month Club founded in 1926 and the Literary Guild founded in 1927, began during the period under study. The Literary Guild presented eleven of the one hundred and forty-five best sellers included here as its recommended first choices.[3] The Book-of-the-Month Club chose twenty-two as its primary selections.[4] Further information is available for the Book-of-the-Month Club. On the average, 60 per cent of the members each month choose to buy an alternate to the recommended selection or no book at all.[5] Furthermore, during the entire life of the Book-of-the-Month Club, roughly thirty times the number of books presented as the primary selection have been offered to club members and descriptions of them provided.[6] It must be concluded then that, while the book clubs do give a certain boost to their selections, they also spread knowledge of the contents of many new books. The clubs do not dictate taste. Rather, the options are presented to the prospective readers and they then choose. The most important role of the book clubs in terms of the goals of this study is that of providing one more source of information to a large audience about new books. In one or more ways, then, the reader does indeed have some idea about the contents of a book before he reads it.

Studies of what makes a particular book a best seller suggest that a combination of factors account for its sales. Frederick Lewis Allen, for example, wrote in 1935 that public acceptance of a book depends on four factors: the author's previous reputation; the publisher's ingenuity and his confidence in the author; the collective judgment of reviewers and booksellers; and the tendency of the book buyer to follow the crowd.[7]

The publisher does play an important role in the success of a book, but it is not simply printed advertising that makes the difference. The best publicity for a book is passed on by word of mouth from a reader to a potential reader. The publisher can begin this chain by convincing the booksellers to read a certain book. If they like it, they will then pass on the recommendation to their customers. Formal advertising expenditures usually follow sales, increasing as sales increase, merely as a booster to the more important verbal campaign.

Lincoln's Doctor's Dog by George Stevens is a case study of the progress of one book, *Anthony Adverse*, to its position as a best seller.[8] Stevens gives primary credit for the success of this novel to the word-of-mouth spread of knowledge of the book, boosted by its original sale to a large number of potential discussants by the Book-of-the-Month Club. Stevens points out that there is no formula for creating a best seller. He invents a classic example. At the time he wrote his book, sales were high for books about Abraham Lincoln, doctors, and dogs. Therefore, he facetiously suggested, the best seller of all should have been written about Lincoln's doctor's dog.

The question of who makes up the reading population is crucial in determining just whose attitudes and values are being reflected by the best sellers. Some studies have been addressed to this question. None of them give complete information about age, sex, region of residence, economic status and educational level for the entire period 1914 to 1945, which would be the optimum, but they do provide some indicators.

In the first place, the reading population is limited. Bernard Berelson did a study in 1951 which is of interest despite the late date of the survey. He found that one half of the adult population of the United States read one book every six months, 25% to 30% one book every month, and 6% to 8% one book a week. He determined that 10% of the adult population did 70% of all book reading.[9] He found that men and women read approximately the same amount and that the wealthier read more than the poor. The young read more than their elders, but, he said, that is probably because they have more education.[10] Always, more education leads to more book reading.

The factor of education means that the reading population of 1951 represented more people than did earlier reading populations. The percentage of illiterates has decreased steadily since 1910 while the number of high school graduates has increased very rapidly, as Table 1 shows.

Table 1

Percentage illiterate in the population[11]

Year	Percentage
1910	7.7
1920	6.0
1930	4.3
1940	2.9

High school graduates[12]

Year	Graduates
1910	156,429,000
1920	311,266,000
1930	666,904,000
1940	1,221,475,000

These educational statistics indicate that the reading population has not only increased but also broadened as education has become available to a wider variety of people.

While there is a correlation between higher economic status and greater reading, readers are not limited to people wealthy enough to be the frequent bookstore patrons. For the period 1919 to 1931 an 80% correlation has been found between book store best sellers and books with the highest library circulation.[13] This would indicate that the most important factor in determining the reading population is education, rather than simply the possession of money enough to buy large numbers of books. This means that the reading population is fairly widely spread through the middle and upper economic classes. To summarize, readers appear to come from the middle and upper classes, fairly evenly balanced between men and women,[14] well-educated, with youth slightly favored.

Residence provides one other factor of importance. Several studies have been done of the geography of reading. These show that the same pattern has continued for several recent decades. Probably the same was true earlier. A study in 1954 revealed some significant statistics.[15] In the United States, two thirds of the counties and one half of the urban places with a population 5,000-10,000 had no good book outlet. Fifty per cent of the places with 10,000-25,000 had no good book outlet. The Northeast region, with 26.5% of the national population, had 42.4% of all book sales in 1946. New York State alone accounted for 22.2% of all book sales in 1944. In that same year, 17 of the states had only 4% of the book sales.

The most thorough study of the geographical factors in reading was published in 1938.[16] This work by Louis R. Wilson shows that the 1954 situation had been true earlier and goes into far greater detail. Wilson found that the public library was the most important factor in the distribution of books. It exceeds bookstores, rental libraries, loans from friends and all other sources. It is, however, sales, not library circulation, that determine the best sellers. There is no conflict here since library circulation and book sales correlate so highly. Wilson found further that libraries, bookstores, rental libraries, magazines and daily newspapers follow the same pattern of distribution throughout the country.[17] That is, all are high or low together. Distribution of books also correlates positively with literacy and mean income by region. The Far West and the Northeast have the highest distribution of books; the Middle West follows third and the Northwest fourth. The Southwest and Southeast rate lowest in distribution of books and also in literacy and income.[18]

These regional findings confirm the general correlation of educational level and income with amount of reading. More highly educated, wealthier people read more. City dwellers read more than do their rural counterparts. Northerners and Westerners read the most, Southerners the least of all. Northeasterners buy the most books thus playing the most important role in creating the best sellers. It would not be fair to say that the best sellers reflect *only* the attitudes and values of middle and upper class, educated, urban residents of the Eastern, Western and part of the Northern sections of the country, but certainly this group is the most highly represented. As the changes in attitudes and values in the novels are analyzed, it will be primarily this select but very powerful group that is being studied.

It is a requirement at this point to define upper, upper-middle, middle and lower class as the terms are used in this study. W. Lloyd Warner in his analysis of *Yankee City* briefly defined social class in the following way:

> By social class is meant two or more orders of people who are believed to be, and are accordingly ranked by members of the community, in socially superior and inferior positions.[19]

In this study only upper, upper-middle, middle, and lower class are used, rather than the six divisions Warner defines. Furthermore, in these stories social classification normally corresponds with economic status. The one exception is that among upper class characters some have high status in a social sense, some are wealthy, and some have both status and money. This is made clear in individual cases. Middle class characters generally are considered average in both social standing and income by the other characters and by themselves. Upper-middle class people are slightly above these in earnings, education, and/or influence and social standing. Characters defined as lower class are portrayed by the authors as poor in a financial sense, and they generally consider themselves to have economic difficulties. As Warner has remarked, there are always some borderline cases,[20] but where those are significant they are discussed individually.

This study of best sellers is based on the following premises. First, most of the readers of the best sellers were educated, middle or upper class residents of the Northeastern, Northern, or Far Western sections of the country, an extremely influential group of Americans. Second, the best selling novels tend to present attitudes and values and contain characters who embody those attitudes and values with which the majority of the readers identify. The changes in the attitudes and values of the readers thus are reflected by the changes in the novels. Therefore, the gradual nature of the change of popular thought and feeling can be described and analyzed by examining changing themes, characterization and styles in these best sellers.

The basic research material for this study is one hundred and forty-five novels that were the best sellers from 1914 to 1945. A list of these is provided in Appendix A. "Best seller" can be defined in several different ways. The variety in definition comes from the differences in treatment of sales figures. Sales figures can be counted in yearly totals or they can be calculated for the total life of a book. The trade magazine, *Publisher's Weekly*, for example, calculates the ten books with the highest sale in the hardback edition through book stores for each year. Alice Payne Hackett has compiled these yearly lists in her study, *60 Years of Best Sellers.*[21] In this she lists the ten leading books in both fiction and non-fiction categories. The difficulty of using such lists is what they omit. Book club editions and reprint editions are not counted. The book club sales usually represent a large number of copies sold close to the date of publication. Reprint editions at a lower cost often follow within only a year or several years after a novel's original publication. These also claim a large number of readers who come from what is basically the same generation, although perhaps a slightly lower income group, than the original buyers. Furthermore, the yearly method of selection tends to exclude the books that come out near the end of the year and thus split their highest sales between the last months of one year and the first months of the next.

Because of the narrow limits imposed by the yearly method,

it seemed better to choose the alternative manner of calculation, choosing best sellers in terms of the book's total sales in *all* editions over its whole life in print. This is the cumulative method. Such a list is found in Frank Luther Mott, *Golden Multitudes,*[22] a study of best sellers from the colonial period to 1945. Mott, in fact, has two lists, defined as follows:

The over-all best sellers in the United States:

> Each book in this list is believed to have had a total sale equal to one per cent of the population of the Continental United States . . . for the decade in which it was published.[23]

The remaining books:

> These are the runners-up believed not to have reached the total sales required for the over-all best sellers.[24]

These two lists have been combined into one for the purposes of this study. The combined list is given in Appendix A. There is a notation made of which books belong to Mott's list of over-all *best* sellers. To qualify for Mott's over-all list, a book had to have the following minimum sale:

1910-1919	900,000
1920-1929	1,000,000
1930-1939	1,200,000
1940-1945	1,300,000

Although the cumulative list includes sales that could have occurred as much as thirty-one years after the original publication of the earliest books, it does include many books that made the yearly lists. Eighty-five of the one hundred and forty-five taken from Mott's lists are also in Hackett's top ten for one or more years. In Appendix A, notation also indicates which books these are. Of the sixty that are not in both lists, only sixteen fall into the category of general novels. Three of the exceptions can be classified as children's books, and two are Westerns. The largest category of exceptions is the mysteries, i.e., those books in which the solving of a crime forms the center of the plot, of which thirty-two of the total forty-two did not make Hackett's list for any one year.

Although the mysteries included in this study were written primarily during the second half of the 1920's and during the

1930's, they had their largest sales in the cheap reprint editions that followed the original edition and have been reissued continuously for succeeding years. Mystery sales appear to be particularly high after 1939 when Pocket Books, Inc., the first mass purveyor of paper backs, was founded.[25] The fact that few mysteries are listed during the 1940's does not mean that there was a decline in the number produced. Rather, this reflects the time lag between the original date of publication and the number of years of cumulative sales necessary to reach the cumulative list. This pattern of gradually accumulating sales is typical for the mysteries. These will be treated in a separate chapter.

For the non-mystery novels, another typical sales pattern exists. The highest sales occur in the first year of publication and somewhat less in those immediately following it. There is a rise again if the book is reissued even much later in a cheap edition. For example, one of the all time greats, *Gone With the Wind*, followed this pattern quite well. In the original hardbound publication it sold 1,123,666 copies in 1937, the first year of publication. The second year it sold 138,810, and the third year 15,129. But in that year, 1939, the first cheap edition ($1.49 instead of the original $3.00) sold 333,663 copies. By 1942, sales dropped to numbers of five digits annually where they have remained ever since. Books rarely continue to sell at such a high level for so long.[26]

The presence of books whose original sales did not qualify them for a yearly list does not alter conclusions drawn in this study about *changing* popular attitudes and values. There are three reasons for this. One is that most of them did have their highest sales within a few years after their publication, so that they represent roughly the same time period. Secondly, many of the books which fall into this category are mystery stories which are treated in a separate chapter. Thirdly, no change in thought occurred so sharply that a difference of one year or several years meant a major transformation of values. This is true in view of the fact that a reading generation lasts possibly for more than forty years, and so there is necessarily an overlap in values. As new generations begin reading, the older ones still reading do not necessarily alter their whole way of looking at the world. Because of this generation factor, the way to find the changes is to look for the appearance of new ideas that grow in strength rather than for the sudden disappearance of the old.

I have rated each book by using two hundred specific items or questions in forty-five major categories of attitudes or underlying values. Each item for each book has been rated on a 0 to 5 scale. The scale has two basic variations: low to high in importance; or negative to positive in the judgment of the leading good characters and, by implication, the author of the novel. The categories rated by both sets of scales include certain stylistic features such as language and types of humor and such technical factors as locale and time in which the book takes place. Attitudes towards political, racial, religious, and economic issues are rated as is also the depth of concern with some questions. The value, positive or negative, placed on such matters as occupation, work as an effort, education, art and nature is rated. Depth of identification with reference groups such as family, community, nation, and mankind is evaluated. The view of family life and social behavior is categorized in the same manner. Underlying values such as religious belief, view of the nature of man, comparison of expectation and achievement levels, degrees of judgments of good and evil, and moral judgments about how life should be lived are also rated. A complete listing of the items and the rating system is given in Appendix B.

With the help of these ratings, I then made comparisons in two directions. Within each book I could see what was considered important or unimportant and what was judged good or bad. As I moved chronologically through the list of books, I found obvious changes in such evaluations.

On the basis of a scale of similarity arrived at from the ratings for each item, the books have been divided by a computer into groups which show the closest internal correlation. It should be emphasized that the only function of the computer was to group the books. This calculation was performed on the basis of ratings made by the author. Four groups were defined by temporal periods: 1914 to 1916, 1918 to 1927, 1928 to 1937, and 1938 to 1945.[27] The fifth group were the mystery stories. I decided to treat these separately for two reasons. The primary reason was that they are more similar to each other than they are to the other books from the period in which they were written. The secondary reason was that the difference in the sales patterns indicates that they represent a set of values which are expressed from the 1930's through to the end of the period studied, 1945.

Needless to say, the analysis is not solely mathematical. The statistics and the comparative ratings provide a certain structure within which to evaluate the books. Characters of fiction cannot be categorized on any 0 to 5 scale. The scale is only a useful tool with which to begin analysis.

In the following chapters, I will do what the computer cannot do, which is to analyze the novels and the changes in attitudes and values which they reveal. In the first part of each chapter, I will present certain statistics about the books of the period and then I will consider the style in which the authors wrote. In the second section of each chapter, I will describe and try to explain the attitudes towards the outside world that are reflected in the novels. This outside world includes matters concerning politics, race, economic class, and other external forces. The final section of each chapter will look inward and review personal relations and personal values which change along with the attitudes towards external affairs and often help explain them. On the basis of this examination, I hope to point out changes in attitudes and values of middle and upper-middle class Americans, particularly those who live in Eastern, Far Western and Northern cities, during the important thirty-one-year period between 1914 and 1945.

CHAPTER 2

1914-1916: THE SIMPLE LIFE

Best Selling Novels: 1914-1916

1914	Edgar Rice Burroughs, *Tarzan of the Apes*
1914	Booth Tarkington, *Penrod*
1914	Harold Bell Wright, *The Eyes of the World*
1915	Somerset Maugham, *Of Human Bondage*
1915	Eleanor H. Porter, *Pollyanna Grows Up*
1915	Gene Stratton Porter, *Michael O'Halloran*
1915	Mary Roberts Rinehart, *"K"*
1915	Booth Tarkington, *The Turmoil*
1916	Eleanor H. Porter, *Just David*
1916	Booth Tarkington, *Seventeen*
1916	H. G. Wells, *Mr. Britling Sees It Through*
1916	Harold Bell Wright, *When A Man's A Man*

The best sellers written during these years before America became involved in the first World War provide a glimpse at a civilization that has now disappeared. The books reveal a naivete combined with a popular unwillingness to move beyond the familiar. The characters in the books and apparently the majority of the readers did come from the old largely Anglo-Saxon middle class. According to Richard Hofstadter, this group was at the end of its Progressive protest against its loss of authority to the newly rich industrialists and the big city immigrant-supported politicians. The impending resignation from the struggle may be indicated by a tendency in the popular literature to turn inward, emphasizing personal and moral superiority and happiness, rather than economic or political concerns. Nevertheless, the fiction of this period is not the literature of embittered losers. The best or leading characters win. Generally each novel presents a microworld of good people. In this world, the occasional villains invariably lose. The goals of the good are achieved.

The novels reflect more accurately Robert Wiebe's idea of a search for order. The order most of the characters turn to lies in the realm of personal morality and personal happiness. And in these areas success is attainable. Order is achieved.

The majority of the novels that were best sellers in the pre-World War I period reveal little or no influence of the writing of the realists and naturalists whose works the intellectuals of the day were reading. The best sellers fall back into the values of romantic writing, which was new in America in the middle of the nineteenth century. Like the earlier romantic novels, the best sellers of the years 1914 to 1916 stress the importance of feeling and intuition, the value of individualism, and the appeal of ingenuousness. Most of the authors of this group of books have not yet begun, by the second decade of the twentieth century, to try to explain individual differences nor do they give much consideration to social causation or larger social questions. If the novels that were best sellers from 1914 to 1916 may be taken as base line representation of the attitudes and underlying values of the American Anglo-Saxon middle class, then clearly those people failed to recognize that America had, indeed, changed since 1890 and before.

The twelve novels which represent this period form the smallest and most homogeneous group in the study. The books written in 1914 are: *Tarzan of the Apes* in which Anglo-Saxon superiority is demonstrated in the African jungle, *Penrod* which is a humorous account of a middle class boyhood, and *The Eyes of the World* in which pure hearts and pure art are proved superior to painting for the sake of making money. The year 1915 brought two more books about children, *Pollyanna Grows Up* and *Michael O'Halloran.* Both involve kindly people rescuing poverty-stricken children. Two stories coupling young love and moralizing also appeared in 1915. These are *"K"* and *The Turmoil.* The following year, 1916, saw the appearance of another book about a helpless child, *Just David*, and *Seventeen* which deals with middle class youth, and another sermonesque novel by Harold Bell Wright, author of *The Eyes of the World*, entitled *When A Man's A Man.* In the latter, the natural quality of the West reveals the manhood or lack of manhood in the male characters. The ensuing analysis will reveal the many similarities of these books. Significantly, the only two best selling novels which do not fit this pattern were written by British authors. *Of Human Bondage* by Somerset Maugham and *Mr. Britling Sees It Through* by H. G. Wells contain more complex characters, problems and solutions than do the American-produced books.

Like the novels, the authors form a fairly homogeneous group. Only two of the authors are foreign, the two British novelists. Of the Americans, authors of five books were born in the Northeast and authors of five in the Middle West. The settings follow the place of birth with the exception of Harold Bell Wright's. He turned to the West to find Nature and thereby purity. These authors were well known to the American reading public, since one of their books appeared as far back as 1899 on Mott's list of best sellers. All except Edgar Rice Burroughs, the creator of Tarzan, had at least one earlier best seller.

The American authors, all born between 1868 and 1875, grew up in the immediate post-Civil War North. Their formative years were those when America was experiencing the rapid growth of big business and the acquisition of fortunes that came with it. As the authors matured, the Populist and Progressive protests came to the fore, and the land experienced a high point of immigration.

The books all have a contemporary setting, with at least part of the plot taking place in the twentieth century. Yet they are set largely in the wilderness, on farms, in small towns or in small cities. Where large cities play a role, they are viewed with distrust. They are shown to be cold at their best, corrupting at their worst. In a time of rapid urban growth, the authors of best sellers and their readers apparently preferred to ignore or turn away from the city.[1]

Stylistically the language is uniformly simple. A fair amount of class dialect is written in, and some use is made of colloquialisms. Regional dialects (most peculiar to the South and the West which are practically unrepresented), foreign words or phrases or technical language occur very rarely and profanity or vulgarisms not at all. The simplicity of the language corresponds with the simplicity of the plots.

There is some humor in all of the books, although it is never prominent except in Booth Tarkington's *Penrod* and *Seventeen.* What humor there is tends to occur in day-to-day interaction, in what are styled as typical human reactions to typical situations, often within the family. Children particularly play the comic roles, and the humor comes from viewing the pranks and emotions of childhood from the adult point of view. Unlike Tarkington, the creators of Pollyanna Whittier, David in *Just David*, and Michael O'Halloran take their children quite seriously. Tarkington further differs from his contemporaries in employing both very obvious ethnic humor and in making fun of individual characters. Tarkington's sharpness points up the blandness in the humor of the other authors.

The technical and stylistic features of this group of books correspond with the authors' general presentation of life. Both are uncomplicated. Both speak for the simplistic conception of the world that was disappearing but which the readers of the pre-war era clearly preferred.

In the novels of this early period, personal themes, and the working out of personal lives and problems predominate over any social theme. The largest social concern expressed in the books is the problem of how to find personal happiness in the contemporary world. The search for happiness involves economic and moral conflicts but the primary concern is still with personal interaction, family relationships and young love.

The best selling novels at the end of the Progressive era reflect little of the political concerns of the reformers. There is no active involvement in politics at any level by any of the leading characters created by the American authors. Only slight consideration is given to any political issue. This holds true for all three levels of possible political involvement: international, national and local. The characters have little feeling of identification with any political unit as a political entity: town, city, state, country or world.

The international sphere receives extremely slight attention.

Despite George Kennan's assertion that after 1900 America recognized its position in world affairs[2] and despite the waging of a great war in Europe, not one of the novels written by Americans on the list studied deals at all with any form of international politics. This probably reflects another difference between the political elite, whom Kennan was writing about, and the middle class reading public. Except for colonial exploiting and cruel sailors who appear in *Tarzan of the Apes* there is no discussion of the military in the novels. There are not even any negative judgments of the world leaders for beginning the war or assertions that reform of the international political system is necessary or desirable. There is no plea for the isolation of America from world affairs. There is simply no interest.

One of the two British products, *Mr. Britling Sees It Through* ("it" being the Great War), goes deeply into the personal and moral factors behind political involvement. Mr. Britling changes his position from an assertion that war just could not come to a belief that God is operating through men to achieve His desire in the world. His son, Hugh, is sacrificed for democratic ideals. Mr. Britling's involvement goes even further. He becomes interested in national politics because of his contact with Hugh's soldier friends who are from the working class. He learns that human values mean more than class and feels that domestic economic reforms must be made after the war. H. G. Wells, through Mr. Britling, maintains that individuals are basically good, but Mr. Britling comes to condemn governments and their leaders for all the ills of the world.

In the American novels, national political questions are of almost as little concern as are the international issues. Gordon Milne, in a study entitled *The American Political Novel*,[3] has picked out the leading concerns of political novels in the early part of the twentieth century. They are three: removal of corrupt influences from national, state and local governments, change in the machinery of government to put the power in the hands of the many instead of the few, and a call for the increase of government power to relieve social and economic distress.[4] This reflects the national Progressive program. But a general concern for these reforms is almost totally lacking in the novels studied here, even though these books did reflect the other, non-political elements of the Progressive ideology.

The only sort of nationalism reflected is a love of everything American, a feeling of unity which allows and makes lovable characters presented as typically American. Although the locales remained predominantly in the East and Middle West, specific real places are rarely named. *Michael O'Halloran, "K"* and *The Turmoil* can take place in any small sized city. Penrod and William and Jane Baxter of *Seventeen* fit as the children in anybody's neighborhood. This is tacitly assumed. The South, notably, goes unrepresented and without mention. It apparently is not included in the realm of the typically American.

Local politics concern the authors only slightly more than do international or national politics. States appear to have no political existence whatsoever. Only two of ten novels touch on local political issues and these involve corruption and the need for reform. Booth Tarkington's *The Turmoil* vaguely shows a connection between industrial men of power and political men of power. Bibbs Sheridan, the sensitive son of the industrialist, toys with socialism as a way to cure the economic injustices. He envisions a change on both a national and a local level, but the basis of his objection is local conditions. Bibbs soon relinquishes ideas of fundamental change in favor of making the existing system work more justly and to the benefit of all the people.

Corruption is specifically mentioned by only one author, Gene Stratton Porter in *Michael O'Halloran.* It appears only incidentally in the person of the politician father of Leslie Winton. After Mr. Winton decides to reform and makes good his debts, newsboy Mickey, a would-be reporter, and his editor conspire to keep the scandal a secret, so Leslie and her fiance can be married with no shame blighting their happiness. Obviously, the basic concern is not political.

Daniel Aaron in *Men of Good Hope* characterizes the Progressives as protesting against a betrayal of the republican ideal.[5] In the novels, there is a slight element of political disapprobation, but the real protest lies in other areas. On a political level, then, the characters obviously are not Progressive types. Stronger emotions are found in connection with ethnic and economic conflicts and attitudes, family life and the religious, moral and personal values in the books written from 1914 to 1916.

The leading characters of the best sellers of the pre-World War I period are all white Anglo-Saxons of unspecified Northern European heritage. Racially, thus, they resemble Progressive types. Only a few minor characters come from Southern or Eastern European, Oriental, American Indian or Negro families. There is little discussion of race or racial issues in either a specific or a generalized context. For the most part, there is an assumption, at best, that white, Anglo-Saxon Protestants want to read only about white, Anglo-Saxon Protestants or, at worst, that people not in this ethnic category are not important enough to be the material of serious literature. Vernon Parrington comes close to describing the actual situation in the pre-war world when he proposes that we never really achieved democracy, only careless individualism that left society at the mercy of the middle class.[6] Gunnar Myrdal counts the essential dignity of man as one of the basic postulates of democracy,[7] yet the minority racial and nationality figures are bestowed with very little dignity in these novels. The extreme degree of emphasis on the middle class in the novels reveals a lack of concern for any other kinds of people, a point which tends to confirm Parrington's suggestion.

The Negro has always been the subject of ambivalent feelings by Americans. In the fiction from 1914 to 1916 these feelings range from a judgment that the Negro is a poor unfortunate who must be cared for to a belief that he is congenitally stupid and definitely possessing tendencies toward criminal violence.

In *Tarzan of the Apes* Burroughs regrets the white man's exploitation of the African natives, but at the same time he makes it quite clear that the apes (perhaps representing some sort of natural order) have a higher morality than do those same natives. Ironically, Tarzan's ape-mother, Kala, receives greater approbation for her love and care for Tarzan than do most non-Anglo-Saxons. The natives inflict a wide variety of barbaric and brutal tortures on their victims. The apes do not. Tarzan, somehow genetically carrying an innate sense of Anglo-Saxon morality, not only recognizes the apes as superior to the black cannibals but lives a definition of what man should be. He is loving of family, intelligent, desirous of learning (he teaches himself to read from an abandoned primer), and responsible to other men even at the cost of relinquishing selfish goals, specifically Jane.

Aside from Burroughs' venture into Africa, only Tarkington's three books contain Negro characters, who appear in comic roles. Tarkington's white children happily refer to black people as niggers and coons. The Negroes all speak in a dialect of bad grammar and mispronunciation. They are lovably picturesque but definitely inferior. Beginning at age seventeen, the yard man in *Seventeen* has fathered numerous children by numerous women, and at sixty-one he does not know where or who they all are. The liveliest of the black characters are Herman and Verman, two small brothers, who are found by Penrod and Sam. Verman is encumbered with a speech defect for which he is made a display in the white boys' show. Herman is an added attraction because he had had Verman chop off one of his fingers with an axe. The little Negroes become faithful allies in Penrod's and Sam's feud with bully Rupe Collins. Verman, without white rules of fair play and with reasonable ingenuity, takes after Rupe with a rake:

> For in his simple, direct African way, he wished to kill his enemy . . . Rupe had not yet learned that an habitually aggressive person runs the danger of colliding with beings in one of those lower stages of evolution where theories about "hitting below the belt" have not yet made their appearance.[8]

Herman and Verman come off as little better than savages. They belong more to the jungle than to America. They are not individuals with thoughts and sensibilities.

Orientals appear only twice in this period. In Harold Bell Wright's *The Eyes of the World*, an oriental servant speaks in dialect. In Maugham's *Of Human Bondage*, "Oriental depravity"[9] is exemplified by an oriental who seduces a German girl. Like Negroes, Orientals are dehumanized and inferior.

Jews receive better treatment than Negroes and Orientals, but they are still singled out as possessing special racial characteristics. In Mary Roberts Rinehart's *"K"* they are differentiated but are accepted on the fringes of the life of the town. They are not included socially, but they are considered people, if stereotyped. In *Penrod* the Jewish boy in town is too rich, often gets only that acceptance that his money will win for him, is something of a sissy and wants to own a big store when he grows up. *Of Human Bondage* shows that the British were capable of the same sort of stereotyping. At Brighton, "There were many Jews, stout ladies in tight satin dresses and diamonds, little corpulent men with a gesticulative manner."[10] Despite these descriptions there is none of the invective that might be expected to follow the beginnings of anti-Semitic discrimination in employment and housing that Oscar Handlin places in the early twentieth century.[11]

All of these racial stereotypes are minor characters, not recognized as individuals, it is true, but treated without hatred. Except for the slight amusement they provide or the casual glimpses of them, they may as well not exist in the lives of the Anglo-Saxon Protestants. They are exterior to their existence. This is dehumanizing to the racial minorities, but active hatred is lacking. Also none of the minorities appear as any threat. This may reflect the fact that none of the American authors came from either the South, where so many Negroes lived, or the Far West, to which the largest number of Orientals had immigrated.

There was even less concern for Southern and Eastern Europeans in the novels. This is despite the high rate of immigration and the fact that the depression of 1914 had resulted in antagonisms between native American and immigrant workers who were in competition for jobs.[12] In 1910 the report of the Dillingham Commission on immigration had been issued. In seeking to rationalize the exclusion of further immigrants from Southern and Eastern Europe, the report characterized them as less healthy, less intelligent, less efficient workers.[13] Despite all the official furor, the only reference to any Southern or Eastern European in America was a brief reference in *Seventeen* to a Dago waiter who cut off a lady's head. To be sure, this is no compliment, but it is the only concern.[14]

The lack of interest in racial matters is consistent with the lack of concern for any but personal problems. The attitude toward the non-Anglo-Saxon members of society is fairly derogatory. There is little sense of any mission to help and still less that all human beings carry an essential human dignity merely because they exist. In the end, racial questions and their implications for democracy are basically ignored. Handlin's idea that economic exploitation and racial prejudice are somehow related[15] is upheld to the extent that minority group members are often servants and shown as being capable of little else. But the overwhelming impression, as in the case of politics, is of remoteness and lack of interest.

Social and economic class of the characters and relationships among the classes play a much more important role in the pre-war novels than do either politics or race. The classes to which characters belong are explicitly defined and their virtues or shortcomings discussed. Not surprisingly, the middle and upper middle classes provide the bulk of the leading characters. Members of the lower social class appear frequently in servant roles and several times as poor children to be helped. There is one criminal who is partially reformed by contact with middle class virtue.[16]

The servants lack great interest or individualization except for the racial stereotyping of Negroes. Only the white maid Tillie in "*K*" really comes alive for the reader, and her circumstances reflect a middle class feeling that morality among the lower class is not as important as it is among those who rank higher. Tillie moves in with a man to whom she is not married. His wife is in a mental hospital and he cannot marry Tillie. Sidney Page and "*K*," really Dr. Edwardes, support her in this venture although Sidney is the type who helps reform a whore. Sidney, a middle class girl, is also explicitly a virgin. Before the end of the book, the hospitalized wife of Tillie's lover dies, just in time to allow Tillie to bear her baby in wedlock. Despite the moral ending, it seems likely that similar behavior would not be allowed by the middle class hero or heroine of the book.

Several impoverished but extremely virtuous children appear, mainly as the recipients of aid from wealthier characters whose happiness is increased by performing this moral service. *Pollyanna Grows Up* and *Michael O'Halloran* provide the best examples. Pollyanna discovers poor and crippled Jamie in the Boston Garden feeding birds and squirrels from his wheel chair. She finally succeeds in convincing the moping rich Mrs. Carew to undertake aid to the boy and his adopted family. Mrs. Carew, in turn, becomes happy and open to the world. Virtue is rewarded and the recipient, his natural goodness given a chance, thrives. Michael O'Halloran, another impoverished victim of circumstance and an orphan, is the hero. He had adopted small crippled Lily, whom he has made his "family." The two are taken care of by an assortment of middle and upper middle class families who all benefit in great gains of happiness. Michael, starvation warded off, dedicates himself to working hard at getting an education so he too can join the great middle class.

Working class people during this period thus are viewed by their betters either as servants or incorrigibles or unfortunate victims of circumstance to be helped or disdainfully left alone according to their apparent desire or ability to join the middle class. The lower class characters themselves either desire to rise to the middle class in which case they respect and emulate their superiors or are lazily resigned to poverty and carefreely go their own way. Some poor characters do rise through a combination of their own efforts and the patronage of richer men, but there are no Horatio Alger type rises from nothing to the pinnacle. Nor do these authors, writing for a middle and upper class audience, give any indication that unionism was on the increase from 1914 to 1917.[17] Nor is it surprising that this is the case.

The presentation of upper class characters varies a great deal. Tarzan's English aristocratic parentage is shown to be responsible for his innate personal nobility. In *Penrod*, the public image of the rich family Magsworth is temporarily damaged by the middle class children to the great delight of their fathers. "Sissy" little Magsworth has made a desperate effort to get into the gang by asserting that a female Magsworth who was just convicted of murder is his aunt. The parents' temporary loss of dignity is enjoyed by all. In *Pollyanna Grows Up*, the middle class girl from a small town shows rich Mrs. Carew the road to happiness and also virtue. In *"K"* upper class Dr. Edwardes is inspired to return to surgery through his contact with a young middle class girl, Sidney Page. Upper class characters in the British novel, *Mr. Britling Sees It Through*, are better accepted than they are in any of the American novels. They are presented as quite human individuals.

The Eyes of the World is the only book which shows upper class people as really bad. The evil in the rich Taine family, however, is not so much a function of their upper class status as it is of their preoccupation with money, material goods and their lack of human warmth and giving and honesty. The good people of the book come from a similar background but have purer, less materialistic standards.

This cold materialism attributed to the rich elicits more criticism than any other economic characteristic. This also occurs in Tarkington's *The Turmoil* in a temporary feud between neighbors representing the impoverished old gentility and the new rich of the growing industrialism which is covering the typical midland city with clouds of smoke. For a long while, the old Vertrees family, with its personal sensitivity and appreciation of the arts, resents the intrusion of the Sheridans. Mr. Sheridan shows that he is a self-made man by his use of incorrect grammar. He works constantly, leaving no time for the finer things of life. But the explanation for this is provided in the novel. The basic factor is one of generations. Bibbs Sheridan, the sensitive son, rejects the industry and money as ugly and materialistic. He falls in love with young Mary next door, marries her, saves her family from degradation and starvation, and takes over the family industry to support his beloved wife. Bibbs, however, inserts a humanism into the business that his father, the man on the make, could not. Tarkington justifies Bibbs' participation in the new industrial world and sets the terms of its acceptance when he makes Bibbs say: "If man would let me serve him, I should be beautiful."[18] In the period 1914 to 1916, these appear to be the only terms on which the old Anglo-Saxon middle class can accept the new industrialism and its people.

The predominance of the old middle class makes it evident that further opinions on occupations and work reflect primarily the view of that group. As for specific occupations, two of the heroes are doctors, in *Of Human Bondage* and "*K.*" Otherwise any middle class profession, if performed with honesty, is acceptable. In *The Eyes of the World*, honest artistic endeavor receives the greatest reward in terms of personal satisfaction, and in Wright's other book, *When A Man's A Man*, the hero must lead the rugged life of a cowboy to prove his manhood before he becomes a ranch owner.

Occupation or business is not a strong basis of identification for the characters in many of the books in this group. In *The Turmoil*, there is the struggle between the old and the *nouveau riche* families and within Bibbs. In *The Eyes of the World*, one of the basic questions is honest versus dishonest art. In two other stories doctors seek to be successful in their job. These are the only cases where occupation is of any importance at all.

Success at one's chosen task is rated of greater importance than the specific occupation. But even this success is presented not in terms of material gain or conquest of other men but rather as a fulfillment of oneself, as the means of becoming a whole man or of giving service. Aaron King chooses honest creation of beauty rather than profitable flattering portrait painting in *The Eyes of the World.* Dr. Edwardes in *"K"* and Philip Carey in *Of Human Bondage* have the privilege of serving mankind in using their medical skill. David in *Just David* will make beautiful violin music for the world to enjoy. And Lawrence Knight in *When A Man's A Man* becomes a full man by being a successful cowboy known as Patches. Most of the conflict here lies within the characters over how to find value in their own lives. Where there is economic or professional conflict, it is all resolved before the end of the novel.

Already the novels reflect a turning away from the Puritan idea that hard work is the determining factor (along with God's will) in material success. Although the effort of work contributes to the achievement of success, particularly in *Michael O'Halloran*, the hard-working newsboy, and *When A Man's A Man*, where Patches needs to prove by the quality of his physical work that he is truly a man, the role of work per se is important in only one fourth of the novels. On the other hand, in three fourths of the novels, the possession of a natural skill is much more important. Even where hard work succeeds, it is always coupled with possession of talent. Generally the work involves the training of a talent already possessed. This assumption of the natural inequality of man is anti-democratic in one sense, but perhaps only against democratic ideology rather than any practice America has ever followed. It is the so-called equality of opportunity that allows the impoverished but skilled Michael to prevail. Furthermore, the skill that is looked up to is not always a money earning skill. Penrod and Jane Baxter are skillful at making mischief. Pollyanna is skilled at cheering people up. Tarzan's natural skill allows him to become a full man interested in love and justice, not in accumulating a fortune. Harold Bell Wright's *The Eyes of the World* specifies a moral element not present in Tarkington's works and not so specific in others'. Aaron King possesses great skill as an artist, Sybil Andres as a musician. Conrad Lagrange is a writer who has prostituted his talent but sees the folly of his corruption. He comments on ambition:

> It must be a noble ambition, nobly controlled. A mere striving for place and power, without a saving sense of the responsibility conferred by that place and power, is ignoble. . . . It is a curse from which our age is suffering sorely, and which, if it be not lifted, will continue to vitiate the strength and poison the life of the race.[19]

Great skill must not be wasted. In *"K"*, the central theme concerns the return of Dr. Edwardes to surgery. The return is necessary because he is talented.

Where hard work is rewarded, it is the by-product of a virtuous goal. The Alger hero as described by Kenneth Lynn does not appear.[20] Individual effort is no longer glorified when the sole result is rising to the top of the economic heap. The pursuit of money is not equated with the pursuit of happiness. And business success is not equated with spiritual grace. Work for work's sake or work for material gain alone is not praised or even condoned. Skill, on the other hand, is coupled with virtue except in Tarkington's books and Maugham's *Of Human Bondage* where there is no particular question of abstract virtue. Even in those, the leading characters are efficient. It is the abstract virtue that is lacking.

Despite the general agreement that work is less important than skill and that skill succeeds only when accompanied by virtue, there is great disagreement on the role of education, the formal training of the skill. Perhaps because of this disagreement education is a major concern in fully one fourth of the books. Formal education is both good and necessary in *Tarzan* and in *Michael O'Halloran.* In *Pollyanna* and *Just David* it is something to be shared with the less fortunate by naturally good people in order to allow them to rise in the world. In *Of Human Bondage* and *Just David*, education is necessary to acquire great competency in a specific area, medicine and violin playing. In the majority of these books, education is viewed as a tool which the good people can use to achieve literate middle class status or to apply to some sort of creative endeavor. Formal education is resisted by Penrod. It is given limited condemnation by Harold Bell Wright in *When A Man's A Man*: Patches, the hero, explains: ". . . education . . . is a benefit only when it adds to one's life. If schooling or culture, or whatever you choose to term it, is permitted to rob one of the fundamental elements of life, it is most certainly an evil."[21] There is a professor in the book who personifies all the bad qualities the author associates jointly with formal education and with the East. Kitty, woman of the West, learns of the corruption when she goes East to school for three years.

> In the new world she was to learn that men and women are not to be measured by the standards of manhood and womanhood–that they were to be rated, not for strength, but for culture; not for courage but for intellectual cleverness; not for sincerity, but for manners; not for honesty, but for success; not for usefulness, but for social position, which is most often determined by the degree of uselessness.[22]

Kitty finally returns to the fold when she rejects the unmanly, effete Professor Parkhill in favor of cowboy Phil Acton.

These attitudes seem to uphold the basic thesis of Richard Hofstadter's book *Anti-Intellectualism in American Life.*[23] Intellectuals are shown as pretentious and effeminate. Moral principles appear to be superior to formal knowledge. But the novels do not go as far as Hofstadter believed people went in disdaining formal education. Specifically they convey the idea that education can give good training and they do not condemn natural excellence as anti-egalitarian.

Furthermore, while formal education is partially distrusted and partially resisted, art is generally viewed favorably–if it comes from the soul. Generally it does, in the judgment of this period's novelists. Art does not receive particular emphasis, but where it does appear, it is good. Harold Bell Wright does not criticize pure art, an outflowing from the heart, as he does education. In *The Eyes of the World,* the purity of art is a central theme. Aaron King saves his soul by deciding to paint woodland scenes in all their beauty rather than painting portraits of rich women in which he must hide their natural ugliness. In *Just David* the child's great ambition is to create beautiful music on the violin, and by the end everyone encourages him in this worthy endeavor.

Art and nature do not conflict with each other but rather appear to have the similar function of being or increasing beauty in the world. Nature is an important concern in one fourth of these novels and a lesser consideration in others. Several times nature comes into conflict with civilization, but it is the conflict as seen by the conservationist, not by the pioneer. In nearly one half of the books, nature possesses qualities for saving souls. It is Godlike. David's father raises him in the wilderness so he will grow up without learning the evils that civilization teaches. Patches grows into a strong man by living a healthy outdoor life on a ranch. Aaron King is purified by his contact with the wilderness. Henry Steele Commager lists loss of contact with nature as one of the characteristic elements of the American twentieth century.[24] While the assertion may be true, the romantic ideal still remained strong before the outbreak of World War I. Nature does not appear in the form of natural resources to be used as the source of material abundance.[25] Nor is nature that element upon which all are trying to impose civilization, although this, as de Tocqueville predicted, has been a continuing theme in American history. The writers of these best sellers saw nature not as a hostile force to be subdued and civilized but as a source of purity and beauty. Moral conservationists at heart, they feared the destruction of this goodness. Here then is one more facet of the anti-materialist ethic which pervades the period or, at least, dominates the concern of the old middle class.

At the end of this survey of attitudes towards the world outside, one fact is most salient. In the novels that sold the best from 1914 to 1916, there is a notable lack of interest in that which is far away or unfamiliar. Only those parts of the external world and the general social condition which affect the characters morally or emotionally receive serious treatment. The authors and their readers generally appear to find social problems uninteresting. Instead, they emphasize more personal matters, and it is these emotional and moral questions that are stressed.

Historian Frederick Lewis Allen characterized the novels of this pre-war period as being essentially home and sugar.[26] One or the other or both epithets describe the whole group with the exception of the two novels imported from Britain. The family is either the central or a major reference point in eleven of the twelve novels, including Maugham's and Wells'. The one exception is *Michael O'Halloran*—and this proves the point. Orphaned the hero has no family, but to be part of one is portrayed as a natural desire and Michael accordingly adopts crippled, also orphaned, Lily who becomes his "family." The family unit generally is a nuclear one encompassing only parents, children, and brothers and sisters. Interest in aunts, uncles, grandparents and cousins is much lower. There is only one severe case of feuding among two branches of a family, in *The Eyes of the World,* and this is portrayed as tragic. The relationships among the members of extended families range from very good to very poor, but there is really little interest in relatives outside of the nuclear family unit.

Of the possible family relationships, the emphasis in the novels of this period is on those between parent and child. This follows naturally from the presence of so many children and adolescents as leading characters. The stories are an affirmation of the desirability of good parent-child relations. Parental authority is at least partly accepted at the end of most of the books. Over a majority of the books terminate with loving relations. At their beginnings, the books show a fairly even distribution along a scale of good to bad. At the end of the stories, however, few families end up with even moderate conflict between parents and children. The reconciliation of feuding parents and children plays a major part in *Michael O'Halloran, Just David,* and *The Turmoil.* Even Tarzan and his ape-mother Kala affirm the preference for mutual love. In Tarkington's comic novels, *Penrod* and *Seventeen,* there are small quarrels humorously treated, but the basic familial love is obvious. *The Eyes of the World* shows the tragedy of unhappy family relations, which result from pure selfishness on the part of all the evil Taines. In *Of Human Bondage*, Philip Carey's cynicism and callousness are revealed to be a fear of emotional commitment, and he attributes the cause of this fear to a lack of parental love. In the end, largely through watching a happy family at home, he overcomes his problem and settles down to begin his own family. Happy family life, incidentally, appears to end all his problems. In this period, of all the possible happy endings to stories, family reconciliations and family beginnings (engagements and marriages) are the most popular.

Interestingly enough, most of the love relationships are premarital. Young love plays an important role in over three-fourths of the books. This attraction usually results in a marriage.[27] On the other hand, the realities of actual marriage are explored only rarely. Even within a marital situation, the tendency is to proclaim the good of the institution without going into the details of its operation. An example of one such proclamation comes in *When A Man's A Man* from the lips of Mr. Baldwin, whose role is primarily that of a father and whose wife is largely invisible:

> You take Stella an' me now . . . We've been happy for over forty year . . . No, sir, 'tain't what a man gits that makes him rich; it's what he keeps. And these folks that are swoppin' the old-fashioned sort of love that builds homes and raises families and lets man and wife work together, an' meet trouble together—if they're swoppin' all that for these here new, down-to-date ideas of such things, they're makin' a damned poor bargain, accordin' to my way of thinkin'.[28]

Beyond this bliss there lies the idea that even if a marriage is a mistake the institution is sacred, and the right thing to do is make the best of the situation. Mary Roberts Rinehart states this explicitly in "*K*" where she allows two of the minor characters to be unhappily wed. In the books by American authors, unfaithfulness generally receives the punishment of failure to attain happiness. With the exception of the maid Tillie in "*K*" whose domestic arrangement is finally legalized, only the British books allow unfaithfulness without punishment or permit pre-marital or extramarital sex. In none of the books is sex described as an action. Even mere acknowledgement of the physical effect of first kisses and touching hair is rare and often awkwardly written.

Outside the institution of marriage, other facets of relations between men and women remain. Men tend to play the central role in the novels of this group with women in secondary supporting roles. Pollyanna is the only female who outranks all the males in her book in importance.

Similarly, in only one book is a female really dominant over a male, and the male's continuing submission is portrayed as rather silly. The character is Tarkington's Willie Baxter who has an obsession for baby-talking Miss Lola Pratt. In Harold Bell Wright's books and in *Mr. Britling Sees It Through*, neither men nor women particularly dominate the other sex but, as in all the novels of this group, their spheres of authority are clearly defined and do not conflict. Women are nowhere pictured as particularly weak, but they are always pure and to be honored. The only realm of difference in the portrayal of women's roles is whether or not they can work or must be restricted to their own household. In four of the books, young women work in several of the early women's professions such as teaching and nursing, but these forays into the world are limited to unmarried women.

Sex is one way to divide people. Another is age. Most of the characters in this group of best sellers are mature adults (often parents), pre-married young people, and children. The elderly and also young married people without families are lacking. Youth predominates. In most of the books there is some tension between youth and age, but this is important only in three of the twelve. In all three of these, the conflict is between a parent and a child. Penrod simply does not want to obey the restrictions his parents place on his actions. In *Just David*, the conflict between the Hollys and their son is described only briefly. The important thing is that they are reunited. Only in *The Turmoil* is the generation gap based on defined and detailed principles. Bibbs Sheridan, for a while, rejects his father's company and capitalist ethic. He becomes reconciled to participation in modern industry only when he sees that it can be a service to the people.

Where conflict between the generations does occur, the result is not youth convincing their elders of the rightness of their position. Nor do they simply dominate. Either there is an equitable reconciliation such as that in *The Turmoil* or the elders dominate in a mild way because of their position of authority, usually parental. For example, Pollyanna will not marry her true love until her aunt gives her permission. Youth is the most admired part of life, but it is a youth which is respectful of its elders.

Distinction of characteristics accompanying age is generally only of contributing importance or less. In several cases, understanding and contentment result from increasing age. This occurs particularly in *The Eyes of the World* where older people instruct the younger in the rewards of honest living. More often the process of aging is seen as harmful and approaching death. Older people live less completely, although sometimes young people can influence this tendency. Pollyanna makes Mrs. Carew come alive as David does the Hollys. But throughout, youth and life are equated. There is no real differentiation in terms of morality. Young and old are equally capable of goodness and badness.

The greatest distinguishing factors of youth are its innocence and its characterization as the time of life when instruction should be received. Less important but frequent in occurence are two opposing judgments of youth: half the books emphasize that it is a time to be envied (Pollyanna's constant happiness) and half show youth as a torture to itself. Sidney Page lost her innocence when she began to work in a hospital and face the real world. Learning of its evils proved a painful experience for her:

> The hospital had taught Sidney one thing: that it took many people to make a world and that some of these were inevitably vicious . . . abruptly Sidney had found the great injustice of the world—that because of this vice the good suffer more than the wicked.[29]

Although Sidney emerges thus painfully from her innocence, Pollyanna, David, Sybil Andres and others never do.

The final quality assigned to youth is physical strength. This is a comparatively minor part of youth, and furthermore physical strength is usually of less than central importance where it occurs, yet it is a more important factor in this period than in any other. Fully one fourth of the books count physical strength as a matter of central concern. Tarzan's physical strength, while less important than his humanization, is one of his main attractions. Penrod and his gang greatly admire physical prowess. And Patches must prove himself a man by performing heavy physical tasks. The similarity between Patches' motives and those of Theodore Roosevelt in ranching in the West and in founding the Rough Riders is unmistakable.

A survey of attitudes towards the world and the practices of living goes far to draw a picture of the pre-war generation. But no real understanding can be achieved without looking at the beliefs, the conscious and unconsciously assumed values underlying their behavior and attitudes. In Western society, the traditional framework for expression of belief has been organized religion. Despite the wide appeal of evangelism at this time, theological religion had been replaced for many by a gospel of rules for living, somehow applying religious principles to everyday life. Although the best sellers show more interest in formal religion during 1914 to 1916 than in any other period in the study, it is an important issue in only one third of the novels. Where religion is a factor, it is, for the most part, accepted either completely including dogma and institution, or is presented as providing the basis of moral beliefs without much interest in the institution of the church. The religion is always Protestant, either by specification or by implication. Characters never go to Mass or to synagogue services. If they go anywhere, they go to church and hear a minister preach.

The church-going practices and references to God make an interesting collection. Pollyanna, whose father was a minister, finds that church gives her happiness and takes Mrs. Carew in order to spread the happiness more widely. God is not referred to. Sidney Page finds the hospital vespers comforting but has no fetish about Sunday church attendance. Bibbs Sheridan and Mary Vertrees go to church to hear the music and because it provides a place where they can be alone together. Penrod goes to Sunday school and steals the dime he was supposed to put in the collection.

Characterizations of God differ as widely as the reasons for church attendance and tend to reflect the earthly interests of the characters rather than any theology or Biblical definition. Michael O'Halloran and his friends see God as the maker of both rich and poor. David fights the non-violin playing Sunday Puritanism of Mr. Holly by telling him: "Your God isn't the same one, sir, for mine loves all beautiful things every day in the year."[30] Harold Bell Wright is interested in the purity of nature and of man in a state of nature. In *When A Man's A Man* he refers to the land in the valley being as God made it and says that a man able to live there must have a soul like the "unstained skies, the unburdened wind, and the untainted atmosphere."[31] In *The Eyes of the World* he makes explicit his belief that men in nature, as God made them, are good but they are corrupted by society.

Christianity and God thus are respected, but in a rather vague way, by most of the American authors. Only in *Penrod* does the author mildly mock the church. Penrod not only snitches the collection dime, but he also makes a fool of the young and somewhat effeminate Minister Kinosling by putting tar in his hat. Penrod and group also invent a game to imitate a traveling evangelist. They chant "Go to heaven. Go to hell," and climb a tree towards heaven and then fall down towards hell. These aberrations are not accepted by the children's elders who are horrified at the performance. The objection, however, is to the behavior and the danger of the neighbors' seeing it, not to the lack of belief.

The only serious discussions and criticisms of religion and God take place in the two books by British authors. While these were read by Americans, their quality of thought is deeper and more complex than it is in the American novels. God and the question of the nature of God move all the way through *Mr. Britling Sees It Through* and World War I. Mr. Britling's secretary Letty, when her husband is thought to have been killed, says that God must be either non-existent or evil to allow such bad things to happen in the world. Mr. Britling's response to this is that God is good but not omnipotent, that theologians have misled men by saying that God is all-powerful, and that this is why men grow disillusioned. His God, rather, is fighting with men against evil. By the end of the book he develops this further to the idea that God fights through men to bring a better world, and he says that events and living fall into place only with God. Beyond his religious belief, Mr. Britling explains that individuals are rational and well-intentioned, that trouble comes from governments and impersonal forces. This evil that exists must be fought by men who understand, and he is writing to help make people understand. None of the American authors created any character with such well-defined doubts as Letty, and neither did they give such a detailed affirmation of belief as Mr. Britling. Protestantism for the Americans appears more a part of the pattern of social mores like children going to school or eating with the fork in the right hand.

Somerset Maugham allows his characters to continue through to the end of *Of Human Bondage* with no affirmation of God. Philip Carey is enraged by the hypocrisy of religion when he first witnesses the doings of evil churchmen. He continues to worry about the matter of religion though until he finally decides that he simply does not have a religious temperament. A philosopher friend of Philip's named Cronshaw criticizes a more theoretical aspect of religion: "It's folly, the Christian argument that you should live always in view of your death. The only way to live is to forget you're going to die."[32] Yet when Philip decides that life has no meaning, it is the same Cronshaw who gives him a carpet which holds the key. Philip, after his enlightenment explains: "As the weaver elaborated his pattern for no end but the pleasure of his aesthetic senses, so might a man live his life. . . . He might make a design."[33]

There is no apparent reason why Americans should read about doubt and theology from foreign authors while not from their own, but such is the case. Although readers had some interest in this approach and apparently understood the questions involved, the majority of the best sellers have no such theoretical discussions or issues. In some, there is opposition between good and bad, but this is always presented in terms of living people and concrete deeds. There are conflicts but over *how* to live, not over the abstract nature of life. Perhaps this is one manifest example of the pragmatic tradition.

Putting aside the foreign books, especially Maugham's, some inferences can be made about the values and the nature of the thought of the American reading public just before the outbreak of World War I. As just noted, there was little theory making. Interest was localized and often limited only to a circle of friends. There was little questioning about the effectiveness of democracy in terms of the masses or of Christian theology in terms of its impact on the events of the world or even the nation. There was a strong sense of morality, but this is reflected by how a character treats the few individuals with whom he comes into contact. There is little evidence of any feeling of the larger moral responsibility which Albert K. Weinberg says helped lead to our entry into World War I.[34] The fictional characters betrayed little sense of broad economic or political responsibility. Their world was fragmented into small groups of friends. The fragmentation is shown not only in terms of responsibility and interest but in the characters themselves. The interaction was, for the most part, limited to families and nearby neighborhood friends. The young lovers emerged out of this latter group.

Several of Tocqueville's observations about American society are borne out in these novels. There existed a certain sort of tyranny of the majority in the refusal to recognize any outside way of life or thought. The leading or "good" characters merely assumed that their way was best. For the most part, there could be little discussion on that point for their good was so terribly good and the bad so frightfully bad. These people, like those Tocqueville observed earlier, believed in the perfectability of man in so far as they felt free to remake people in their own image. There was the unpersecuting intolerance of excluding all that was different and not remakable.

One of the basic paradoxes of one sort of Progressivism is reflected in these novels: while society as a whole was blamed for the evils that exist, the solutions were sought only through individuals for individuals. The Reform Darwinist idea that men should plan society was not reflected here. These characters were impotent as far as society went. But there was a sense of a natural leadership and an affirmation that these people would prevail. The "good guys" always won, but the winning appears predestined because they were good rather than the result of planned action.

The mood was optimistic but with a subdued quality because of its narrowness. If one can speak of an impotent optimism, it was here, also a very carefully limited confidence which excluded all that might be defeating or negative from its consciousness. The characters peopling these novels were living with the certainty of ostriches. Inside their tight existence they were sure of themselves, but there was a whole outside world that was ignored. Virtue and social problems were personalized. Responsibility and concern appeared only when a problem was reduced to a personal level.

The personal, narrow world is very much like the world of a child. A young child lives in a comparatively limited and protected community, his society being family and a few friends. Problems of action and decisions about good and bad all come on this personal level. This is very similar to the approach in the novels that had the most readers in America before our entry into the world war. The naivete, the clear cut division between good and bad, the practices of society accepted just because they were there, the unwillingness or inability to see problems in a broader than personal context all mark American readers of popular novels as still comparatively childlike. They had not yet matured with the sophistication of theoretical thought or meaningful concern and action in a wider than personal context.

CHAPTER 3

1918-1927: EXOTICISM, REBELLION, AND SEARCH

Best Selling Novels: 1918-1927

1918	Vincente Blasco Ibanez, *The Four Horsemen of the Apocalypse*
1918	Edward Streeter, *Dere Mable*
1919	Harold Bell Wright, *The Re-Creation of Brian Kent*
1920	Zane Grey, *The Man of the Forest*
1920	Sinclair Lewis, *Main Street*
1920	E. Phillips Oppenheim, *The Great Impersonation*
1921	Dorothy Canfield, *The Brimming Cup*
1921	Zane Grey, *The Mysterious Rider*
1921	Edith M. Hull, *The Sheik*
1921	A. S. M. Hutchinson, *If Winter Comes*
1921	Rafael Sabatini, *Scaramouche*
1921	Edith Wharton, *The Age of Innocence*
1922	Emerson Hough, *The Covered Wagon*
1922	Sinclair Lewis, *Babbitt*
1923	Gertrude Atherton, *Black Oxen*
1923	Rafael Sabatini, *The Sea Hawk*
1924	Edna Ferber, *So Big*
1924	A. A. Milne, *When We Were Very Young*
1924	Anne Douglas Sedgwick, *The Little French Girl*
1924	P. G. Wodehouse, *Jeeves*
1925	John Erskine, *The Private Life of Helen of Troy*
1925	Margaret Kennedy, *The Constant Nymph*

1925 Anita Loos, *Gentlemen Prefer Blondes*
1925 Christopher Wren, *Beau Geste*
1926 Warwick Deeping, *Sorrell and Son*
1926 Thorne Smith, *Topper*
1927 Sinclair Lewis, *Elmer Gantry*
1927 Thornton Wilder, *The Bridge of San Luis Rey*

The best sellers of the post-war period show a marked change from the narrow world view presented just earlier. Horizons have widened geographically and in terms of the variety and complexity of personality and experience. The characters in the novels have become cosmopolitan in their mixture of nationalities, races, and classes. One type of person no longer dominates, nor is there any generally accepted code of values. In fact, a recurring theme in many of the books is the search to find out what really *is* of value. This sometimes begins with exoticism and the escapism of international fantasies and at other times takes place within a more familiar environment.

The greater variety in geographic areas used as settings corresponds to an increase in variety in the character of the people portrayed. Their characters are no longer predictable stereotypes, nor do they always agree with each other. The novels no longer present solutions by which everyone necessarily lives happily ever after. The multiplicity of the values held and of the types of characters given important roles in these best sellers indicate that the readers accepted this new variety. Furthermore, people different in background, life style, and belief from the readers are accepted as being of interest and value as individuals. The search for meaning unites them all.

This search for meaning is not in imitation of a more intellectual literary style. Unlike the writers of the pre-war period, those of this decade have responded to their situation with their own style. Moreover, unlike their more pessimistic contemporaries, most of the writers of best sellers did not give in to disillusionment nor did they accept the feeling of lack of mastery of their own lives so strong in the naturalist writers. The authors of and characters in this best selling group, on the contrary, seem enthusiastic about and excited by a new sense of freedom. The seeking of the twenties, often presented as scatter-brained or as a seeking after sensation, provided the necessary maturing for the people who would soon have to assume social responsibility and world leadership.

The best sellers for the years 1918 to 1927 can be divided into groups which themselves illustrate the variety in what people were reading. Some still followed the pattern of the pre-war best sellers, but these all appeared in the early part of the decade, and this group consists of only four out of the total twenty-eight novels. They are: *The Re-Creation of Brian Kent, The Man of the Forest, The Mysterious Rider,* and *The Covered Wagon.* Three of these four are Westerns, giving a traditional setting for traditional values.

The two books that appeared in 1918 are explicitly war books: Vincente Ibanez's *The Four Horsemen of the Apocalypse,* a serious study of war and its affects on people, by a Spanish author, and Edward Streeter's *Dere Mabel,* a folksy collection of letters by a private to his girl. The war also played a role in the stories of a number of books that cannot be considered primarily war novels.

One obvious result of the war was a new interest in Europe and an acceptance of Europeans as real human beings. A number of novels are about British or Continental characters. Often these are written by foreign authors, or are concerned with the differences between American and European society and mores. In this group are: *The Age of Innocence, Black Oxen, The Little French Girl, The Constant Nymph, Sorrell and Son, If Winter Comes,* and *Jeeves.*

A related group of books can be classified as the exotic novels. These all have foreign settings but also involve spying, piracy, searches for extremely valuable stolen jewels, and similar quests. This group consists of: *The Great Impersonation, The Sheik, Scaramouche, The Sea Hawk, The Private Life of Helen of Troy,* and *Beau Geste.*

The war was followed not only by a greater cosmopolitanism but also by a heightened interest in analyzing the American society which many people had thought they were defending during the war. This analysis of contemporary America, its values and mores, marks still another group of novels. This includes Sinclair Lewis's three best sellers: *Main Street, Babbitt,* and *Elmer Gantry,* and also *The Brimming Cup, So Big, Topper,* and *Gentlemen Prefer Blondes.*

Two books fall into none of the above categories. A. A. Milne's *When We Were Very Young* is a children's book set in England. Thornton Wilder's *The Bridge of San Luis Rey* is a sophisticated study of spiritual meaning in a complex world, a world which most of the authors find interesting, but which this author seems to feel has lost its sense of values. His quest for religious meaning is more searching than any of the pre-war books except *Of Human Bondage* and cannot be considered a return to religious simplicity.

Unlike the group of novels from the years 1914 to 1916, neither the post-war novels nor their authors form a small, homogeneous group. The authors came from widely spread geographical backgrounds. Nine authors are foreigners. Over one-third of the books of the twenties were written by foreigners, a one hundred per cent increase over the former period. Furthermore, the American authors represent all areas of the country, although Middle Westerners and Northeasterners still dominate. Interestingly enough, authors of nine of the books come from the Middle West, authors of five from the Northeast (these sections were equally represented before), authors of two from the Far West, and there is even one who was born just barely in the South—Thorne Smith of Annapolis, Maryland.

As before, a majority of the books are set in the area in which the novelists were born, with the additional proviso that five Americans set at least part of their stories in Europe, one Northerner wrote about the South, and six Easterners and Middle Westerners wrote about the West. In all, fourteen have European, African or Latin American settings. Of the domestic locales, six are Northeast; only one is South; and the Middle West and Far West rate four each.

This group of authors had not achieved the same reputation as had the previous group of authors. Only twelve had earlier best sellers, including all the ten top yearly sellers listed in Alice Payne Hackett's *60 Years of Best Sellers.* The reading public was apparently more willing to read the unknowns.

The authors of the 1918 to 1927 group of books were born between 1857 and 1897. They thus had a much wider range of experience than the best-selling writers of the previous period who were all born within seven years of each other. The writers of these post-war novels grew up from the time of Reconstruction, rapid industrialization and urbanization, through the period of Progressive reform and broadening of international concerns after the Spanish-American War. Although some of the authors were still quite young when World War I broke out, all had reached maturity.

Not only did literary horizons become more international in this period, but the focus of interest turned to the cities. Eleven of the books involve action in urban areas. Some of the newer generation of both writers and readers now accept the large city and approve of its way of life. Small cities declined most in interest, only one being represented. Seven books take place in towns, six on sorts of farms, ranches or country estates, and in six at least part of the action takes place in an undeveloped area such as forest or desert. Exotic settings have increased importance than in the more home-oriented novels of the pre-war period.

The time of action, as well as the setting, varies more during the twenties than earlier, stretching from contemporary times all the way back to ancient Greece for the farce of *The Private Life of Helen of Troy*. Possibly distant historical and geographical settings made the presentation of less conventional action more acceptable.

Style is also more varied. Whereas most of the earlier books are written in straightforward, fairly simple prose, more in this group employ sophisticated language. There is also a marked increase in the use of both colloquialisms and foreign words and phrases.

Humor adds another element of differentiation. It is strongest in the mid-twenties, being of major importance in five of the twelve novels published from 1924 to 1926. Around this same time, humor ceases to be centered around family and children and occurs more in the form of attacks on certain contemporary values or making fun of individual characters and their idiosyncracies. Much of the humor in Thorne Smith's *Topper*, the story of Cosmo Topper and his encounters with the ghosts Marion and George Kirby, comes from his getting in trouble with the authorities and representatives of convention when the ghosts get him into irregular situations. In Anita Loos' *Gentlemen Prefer Blondes*, the blonde happily flaunts both the law and conventional values. After returning from a trip to Europe, she tells everybody that she carried some uncut diamonds, a gift from a man friend, in her handbag so she would not have to declare them at customs. Later, after rejecting the suit of a member of a prominent Philadelphia family, she comments: "I am beginning to think that family life is only fit for those who can stand it."[1] In *Jeeves,* P. C. Wodehouse's humor is based on the famous butler's ability to undo the problems caused by the stupidity of his employer, Bertie Wooster, and Bertie's friend, Bingo. This sort of humor is far removed from the adult view of childhood innocence and pranks on which so much of the pre-war humor was based.

Not only the presence of greater variety in setting, time, style, and kind of humor, but the nature of that variety indicates a more dynamic, more moving era than that before the war. There is a definite increase in energy and a greater liveliness of interest in new and wider phases of life. The differences are in both action and belief. Just how the areas of specific interest or belief are similar to or different from those of the pre-war years will be seen in the ensuing analysis.

Looking outward into the world, the writers and the characters they created both saw a lot that they disapproved of. They made some direct criticisms and many very precise observations. Most often, they merely exercised their freedom to flaunt those traditions and obligations that they felt were left over from an old world outside themselves.

The crucial international political event of the period, World War I and its aftermath, led initially to stories about the war, expressions of patriotic feelings of repulsion from the war and admiration for heroism. They contain further apparent contradictions in that some present a negative view of Europe and others a favorable view of foreign places.

The two books written in 1918 are representative of two kinds of reactions to the war and show the extent that it dominated this first year of the period under review. *The Four Horsemen of the Apocalypse* (they were Plague, War, Hunger, and Death) shows the physical horrors and the emotional sadness of the destruction and dying. The family of Don Marcelo Desnoyers, born a Frenchman, had been in Brazil until the war broke out. Desnoyers then was drawn home to his native country as his German brother-in-law was to his. The family split. Desnoyers' son Julio is killed. Early in the book, the Spanish author Vincente Blasco Ibanez makes a contrast between the New and Old Worlds through the lips of Desnoyers' original employer in Brazil:

> . . . we must recognize that here life is more tranquil than in the other world. Men are taken for what they are worth, and mingle together without thinking whether they came from one country or another. Over here, fellows do not come in droves to kill other fellows whom they do not know and whose only crime is that they were born in an unfriendly country . . . [sic] Man is a bad beast everywhere, I know that; but here he eats, owns more land than he needs so that he can stretch himself, and he is good with the goodness of a well-fed dog. Over there, there are too many; they live in heaps getting in each other's way, and easily run amuck.[2]

Some Americans came to have an equally negative view of Europe as they thought of their men killed in a war that they felt had no positive meaning for America.

Even when there was not much criticism of European corruption, as compared to American purity, strong pro-Americanism in terms of support for the fighting men was mandatory. The homey presentation of a very common soldier's life in *Dere Mabel* by upper class author Edward Streeter demonstrates the degree of interest in the Army men. Even lower class people were important because they fought in the war. The combination of strong conscious American identity and denigration of things foreign is one starting point for thought about international politics during the twenties.

Americans seemed to identify with British patriotism as well as American. Several books published in the few years following the war contain expressions of patriotic feelings about England. *The Great Impersonation* is a spy intrigue where the hero is English and the villain German, but Germany is only mildly condemned. The Kaiser is portrayed as harsh and militarist, but the German ambassador to England is a good man. Discussion of international issues remains at a minimum. The war also plays a part in *If Winter Comes*. Men fight for their country and hero Mark Sabre is unhappy because the Army will not accept him. Yet the love story is the central concern and, in the end, Mark marries his real true love Nona who has not been left in permanent, downcast widowhood after her husband is killed in the war. *Sorrell and Son* gives the only discussion of the war written after 1922, but here the issue is the plight of the veteran whose job and wife both disappeared while he was away–not the war itself. World War I enters significantly into only two of the American books besides those written in 1918. These are both by Sinclair Lewis. In these, the real interest is in the effect on domestic life. By 1920, the publication date of *Main Street*, Carol Kennicott is allowed to be glad that her husband does not have to join the army and is chosen instead to remain as one of the town doctors. Aside from these references to the war, international political questions receive slight treatment during the post-war period. What revulsion to the war there was, was expressed largely by avoidance rather than criticism.

This avoidance of discussion of world political questions was simultaneous with the growing internationalization of characters and non-political subject matter. Despite the negative expression of revulsion to the war, there is one indication that perhaps the judgment of war was not as harsh among the general public as it was among the disillusioned intellectuals. This indication comes from the presentation of military men in the best sellers. Soldiers and fighters of other sorts are involved in over half of the novels, if one includes the actions that took place as far afield as the African desert in *The Sheik* or aboard the pirate ship of *The Sea Hawk.* Judgment of military services generally concedes their necessity in the world. Six of the books present armed strength and soldierly heroism in a very positive manner. Three show military action as necessary without passing judgment on it, while two show it as evil but still necessary. Only three out of the total twenty-eight books in the group portray it as both evil and ineffective. Such characters as Marise Crittenden in *The Brimming Cup* and Dirk DeJong in *So Big* saw the war as a disillusioning experience. Far more characters were admired for military-type virtues. Giles Bradley is admired by the other characters in *The Little French Girl* for his having fought in the war. Beau Geste is admired for surviving the French Foreign Legion. The manly virtues of Sir Oliver Tressilian when he commands a pirate ship in *The Sea Hawk* are shown as making him attractive.

Beyond this approval of manly action in war, an additional factor indicates that there was not as much hostility towards Europe among middle class readers as some historians have suggested. The reading, and therefore, one assumes, acceptance of a number of European authors suggests an acceptance of Europe. So does the setting of so many of the stories in Europe. Even stronger proof comes from the presentation of the European characters in the novels. They are rarely discussed in terms of any inherent difference between Europeans and Americans. Where such a distinction is made, European civilization is often complimented. Europeans are not stereotyped as corrupt people. Miss Loos' blonde in *Gentlemen Prefer Blondes* finds all Europeans quaint and not as anxious to give her diamonds as are American men. In this and in other novels Europe is shown to produce more mature individuals, be they Europeans or Americans living in Europe. These individuals are often women who are shown as less puritanically moral because they have affairs. They are also portrayed as being superior to their American or, in one case, English counterparts, because they understand more of the complexities of life and depths of feeling. In *The Age of Innocence* European-dwelling Ellen Olenska is the real love of American Newland Archer. Her wisdom, interest, and kindness are all superior to that of his American wife. In *Black Oxen*, heroine Marie Zattiany, another American abroad, and her European friends, have greater experience and a profounder knowledge of the world than the American characters have. She too is loved for this by an American man. In *The Little French Girl*, all the characters acknowledge differences between the French and the English which they describe as racial. The French woman, Mme. Vervier, has love affairs, which the English mostly disapprove of, but she too turns out to be a kind and loving and sophisticated person.

The major protest against international politics as with war takes the form of ignoring it. Throughout this period, identification by the fictional characters with either the world at large or mankind as a whole is very low. The attitude is neither bitter nor scornful but rather removed and disinterested. The lack of political or universal interest is similar to that before the war.

National politics continues to be dealt with in the same way international politics are. They are largely ignored. Where minor interest occurs, the attitude is most often mildly critical. The two most seriously put comments on domestic politics form part of Sinclair Lewis' re-creation of town life in the Middle West in *Main Street* and *Babbitt.* Both contain characters that demonstrate a loss of tolerance of differing political points of view. Each book has its non-conformist of whom the town disapproves and deserts because his views are different from theirs. This happens despite the fact that both non-conformists are shown as good, humane individuals. Membership in the Republican party is almost mandatory. For the townspeople, conformity is what counts—not issues. Local and national politics appear as equivalents. The only other comment on American politics can be found in *Topper.* Cosmo Topper's vague proper Republicanism at the beginning is contrasted with his later attitude towards the town functionaries who appear dull and petty when they become involved with Topper and the various offenses committed in the confusion resulting from the presence of his friends the ghosts, Marion and George Kirby.

The decade of the twenties witnessed red flag parades, the Great Red Scare, the Boston police strike, the Harding scandals, the Ku Klux Klan, and the debates between intellectual liberals and conservatives, but little of this excitement is reflected in its most popular literature. Nor is there any sign of a lingering Progressive conscience. There is no longer the preaching for moral regeneration that was present in the earlier novels. Parrington's idea that careless individualism dominates over democratic ideals seems to hold truth here. Henry F. May has noted that the old "idealistic cement" had vanished, that after World War I it was difficult to find a spokesman of the pre-war faith.[3] Not only is no theory on which to base political action promulgated, no author or even character created who appears very interested in theory of government, but even the idea of moral regeneration has also disappeared. The lack of emphasis on politics during the post-war period could reflect two possible different feelings. One could be a lack of interest or a decision that the whole business was too corrupt to meddle in. The other would be a feeling that the individual had no power to affect the procedures of the political establishment. The lack of discussion of the issues could, thus, have reflected a feeling of impotence rather than irresponsibility. Yet, in the end, resignation of power and refusal to take responsibility are two sides of the same thing.

Just as there was little interest in political action, there was little discussion of a democratic credo or of the question of majority and minority rights. Small consideration is given in these novels to the status of minorities and to questions of race and nationality. There is neither widespread hostility to non-Anglo-Saxon groups nor very much assertion of minority rights which some protested were being dismally ignored.

This point may have significance since the early twenties marked a high point of nativism in the United States. Immigration was restricted in 1921 and further in 1924. Until 1925, the Ku Klux Klan grew in the Middle West, North, and Far West as well as in the South, with a large part of its support based on an anti-foreign, anti-Catholic program. During this same time anti-Semitism reached a new high point with the appearance of discrimination in employment and housing and by educational institutions.[4]

The changing middle class opinions of the various minority groups were reflected in the fictional treatment given to them. From 1919 through 1924, most of the books follow the pattern of the pre-war period in that the characters were primarily white, Anglo-Saxon, Protestants. The books with foreign settings involve Western Europe. Even the great desert sheik, the symbol of exoticism and romance to many women of the twenties, turns out to be not a real Arab but rather the offspring of English and Spanish nobles.

In the twenties, as always, Negroes formed the most noticeably different group in America. Fictional treatment of them changes as the period progresses. They become increasingly humanized. In 1918, Bill, who writes letters to Dere Mabel, talks about "Niggers." So does poor white Judy in Harold Bell Wright's 1919 book, *The Re-Creation of Brian Kent.* All the Negroes in that book are servants, but the more educated characters do not call them derogatory names. By 1921, a character appears, Mr. Welles in *The Brimming Cup,* who decides to spend his retirement years in Georgia helping the Negroes. He explains to his surprised friends that Negroes should fight for their own political rights and says further that they cannot fight for their dignity without losing it. He therefore commits himself to this fight. This is the first statement of concern for Negroes in best selling novels. The trend continues in 1922 in *Babbitt* where Sinclair Lewis satirized the bigoted middle class man who says:

I don't know what's come over these niggers, nowadays. They never give you a civil answer. . . . They're getting so they don't have a single bit of respect for you. The old-fashioned coon was a fine old cuss—he knew his place—but these young dingos don't want to be porters or cotton-pickers. Oh, no! They got to be lawyers and professors.[5]

The context makes it clear that Lewis takes strong exception to this point of view. Even the blonde in *Gentlemen Prefer Blondes,* who felt that Europeans were quaint, asserts in 1925 that people should say Negro instead of Nigger because Negroes "have their feelings just the same as we have."[6] And *Topper*, in the following year, gives mild approval to a romance between a mulatto maid and a white stable boy. Here then may be the first signs of recognition in the popular novel that Negroes are real people in possession of some qualities other than the capacity and desire to perform menial tasks for the whites.

Similarly, most of the portrayals of Jews do not uphold any stereotype. Only in *The Sea Hawk* is anti-semitism (by Arabs and Spaniards who believe the Jews to be greedy) accepted without comment. Sinclair Lewis tries in *Main Street* to point out the absurdity of connecting Jews with Communism. In *Elmer Gantry* he characterizes Klan members and other haters of Jews, Negroes and foreigners as evil men. Margaret Kennedy in *The Constant Nymph* comes at the problem from the opposite direction by creating a Jew, Jacob Birnbaum, who is tired of his money and wants love. When he gets that, he and his new wife use his money to help everybody else.

Despite the increased humanization of Negroes and Jews, southern and eastern Europeans continue to be ignored in the best sellers. After *The Four Horsemen of the Apocalypse,* where the main characters emphasize their Europeanness, Latin Americans appear in the novels only in *The Bridge of San Luis Rey.* This book is remarkable for its treatment of Latin Americans, even those with Indian blood, as individualized people.

Rarer types such as North American Indians and Orientals do not appear at all. Two books, *The Sheik* and *The Sea Hawk,* contain Arabs. In both books, they can either embody European virtues or be ruthless and dirty. To be acceptable, they must be European in every way except nationality.

Although the post-war period began with an increase in racial discrimination, a quick if rather feeble voice of opposition grew and was accepted in the popular literature. This does not indicate an era completely lacking in idealism or as unconcerned with the problem of a tyranny of the majority as the writing in pre-war best sellers suggested. Here then is the beginning of an assertion of old and possibly latent values concerning the oneness of man, the beginning of a consciousness that people who are not Anglo-Saxon Protestants are also individuals and that all men possess first humanity and only secondarily race. Certainly the main interest was elsewhere, but some part of the individualist assertion of self in the twenties recognized that other people had an equal right to their individual humanity. Although this assertion is primarily verbal and not in actions directed against discrimination by the fictional characters, this is a beginning in this one area, a beginning which will be seen to occur in other areas as well, of an assertion of mastery over conditions instead of submission to them. The characters now feel that they can challenge customs that are accepted by their contemporaries. This and other similar displays of strength tend to refute John Chamberlain's pessimistic view that after World War I progress gave way to drift.[7]

Class, as a social division, plays a less important role in the novels of the twenties than it did before the war. On the other hand, *possession of money* has become more important to members of all social classes. There are no important contrasts made, as there were in the earlier novels, between the impoverished but genteel upper class and the wealthy but crude nouveau riche. Money and prosperity have become generally accepted as good things. Whether the story involves somehow earning enough money to survive as does *So Big* or whether the money is undiscussed but obvious because of a character's ability to pay for a safari in Africa as Diana Mayo does in *The Sheik,* or whether the acquisitive instinct is overt as it is with the blonde who collects diamonds from men, it is the spending power involved, not social standing, that is of central interest. Money is valued mainly as a way of purchasing excitement and experiences. Frederick Lewis Allen makes the point in *Only Yesterday* that the prosperity of the twenties compensated for the loss of the old idealism:

> What if bright hopes had been wrecked by the sordid disappointments of 1919, the collapse of Wilsonian idealism, the spread of political cynicism, the slow decay of religious certainty, and the debunking of love? In the Big Bull Market there was compensation . . . when the American looked toward the future of his country . . . he envisioned an America set free from poverty and toil. He saw a magical order built on the new science and the new prosperity.[8]

Allen characterizes the prosperity as a new kind of optimism substituted for the old.

Roughly half of the books of this group have leading characters that must be counted as members of the monied class. The greatest frequency of this occurrence falls between 1921 and 1925. This is the period of novels in which rich Americans came in contact with Europe as they do in *The Age of Innocence* and *Black Oxen* and when Englishmen, who appear to be similar to Americans, travelled to Europe and Africa as they do in *The Little French Girl, The Constant Nymph, The Sheik,* and *Beau Geste.* In *Beau Geste*, a missing very large sapphire causes the whole movement of the plot. The adventure and exoticism allowed by the possession of wealth provide the key to the importance of money. Upper class characters who remain in their tight little world at home, like May Welland Archer who is a drag on her more sensitive husband throughout *The Age of Innocence,* are portrayed as not only dull but also destructive to the more feeling and more exciting characters in the books.

The post-war books reflect less interest in average, middle class characters than there was before the war. They appear significantly in only half rather than two-thirds of the novels. Where middle class characters do appear, they take on two basic forms. Some are leftovers of the older, virtuous hard-working simple type. These appear in the three Westerns, Zane Grey's *The Man of the Forest* and *The Mysterious Rider,* and Emerson Hough's *The Covered Wagon* and also in Harold Bell Wright's *The Re-Creation of Brian Kent.* All of these books were written by 1922. *The Mysterious Rider* is typical of the stories and demonstrates other carry-overs from the pre-war period. Strong, hard-working cowboy, Wils Moore, loves the boss's adopted daughter, Columbine.

She returns his love but feels it is her duty to marry another man. Outside interference, like the hand of God rewarding the good, makes her Wils's because that is right. He will inherit the ranch which he deserves because of his hard work and skill and basic goodness.

The other form taken by middle class characters was new and unfamiliar in the pre-war period. These characters are questioning the worth of the style of life that was so widely accepted in the earlier novels. The acceptance and rejection of middle class values varies, but even the question is significant because it is new. It occurs in all of Sinclair Lewis's novels and also in *The Brimming Cup* and *Topper.* These books span the period. Lewis's description of Gopher Prairie in *Main Street* depicts fairly well his presentation of all small city and town middle class societies. The town is presented through the eyes of Carol Kennicott, wife of a doctor and therefore in the upper middle class of Gopher Prairie:

> Carol's small town thinks . . . in cheap motor cars, telephones, ready made clothes, silos, alfalfa, kodaks, phonographs, leather-upholstered Morris chairs, bridge-prizes, oil-stocks, motion-pictures, land-deals, unread sets of Mark Twain, and a chaste version of national politics.
>
> With such a small-town life a Kennicott or a Champ Perry is content, but there are also hundreds of thousands, particularly women and young men, who are not at all content. The more intelligent young people (and the fortunate widows) flee to the cities with agility and, despite the fictional tradition, resolutely stay there. . . .
>
> It is an unimaginatively standardized background, a sluggishness of speech and manners, a rigid ruling of the spirit by the desire to appear respectable. It is contentment . . . [sic] the contentment of the quiet dead, who are scornful of the living for their restless walking. It is negation canonized, as the one positive virtue. It is the prohibition of happiness. It is slavery self-sought and self-defended. It is dullness made God.[9]

Carol leaves Gopher Prairie and her husband and spends several years in Washington, D.C. But, in the end, she returns to the safety and familiarity of her home, husband, and friends.

Similarly, Babbitt asserts that he sees the meaninglessness of life in Zenith with its social snobbisms and sometimes crooked business methods but, like Carol Kennicott, he can find no other satisfactory place to which to turn. In the end, Lewis's indictment is of a way of life not of the individuals whom he portrays as the victims, trapped by the overwhelming norm.

Dorothy Canfield in *The Brimming Cup* creates a woman character, Marise Crittenden, who faces the same sort of questions. After the excitement of first love has worn off for Marise and her husband Neale, she decides she hates the dullness of life as a housewife in their small town in Vermont. The conflict between the traditional values based on family and those of the so-called modern woman in a world of art, excitement and romance is spelled out. As she is about to run off with a rich playboy, Marise changes her mind and remains with the traditional, not because of convention but because life with the husband and children she loves is what she really wants. Here is the counterview to the exoticism of so many of the novels centering around upper class characters that so many middle class people were reading.

There are however middle class characters who do not subside completely back into the inhibitions and routine once they experience something else. The story of Cosmo Topper and his adventures with his ghost friends, the Kirbys, is told as a farce, but the point is deadly serious. After Marion Kirby has led Topper through a series of crazy escapades, he tells her that she has made a new man of him, that he will never be the same man again. She replies, making clear the point of the book:

> You never were . . . life gets you, life and the economic urge—success, esteem, safety. How many of our triumphs in life spring from negative impulses, the fear of losing rather than the wish to win. . . . And no one alive today is to blame. We must thank the ages past and bow to their false gods. . . . We must just keep on and on until the mountains themselves crumble from nausea or we learn to scale them and cool our hands in the sky.[10]

Despite the somewhat resigned tone, Topper has learned how to live and the reader is left with the feeling that he will continue to do so.

The two central themes about class in this period of the twenties at first appear contradictory. The first stresses the use of wealth. The second questions the value of the average middle class way of pursuing that wealth and organizing life according to the tenets of others similarly engaged. Yet behind both of these lies a common search for life—excitement, real depth of feeling and experience. This search is carried out by the individual and for the individual. The characters of the novels do not give central consideration to any broader class structure.

The endowment of conscious individualism in the characters carries over to what portrayal of the lower social classes there is. To be sure, some stereotyped servants perform their duties in the houses of the rich, but no idealized impoverished waifs appear to be acted on by their benevolent betters. The economic-social conscience does not appear to be as strong as it was before the war, but characters with little money become real people instead of stand-ins for helpless if energetic puppies.

The first character from an obviously lower class background who is not pushed upward to middle-classhood is Bill, the rookie soldier, who writes letters to Mable. Granted that because of his poor grammar he was probably laughed *at* more than he was sympathized with, at least Bill's existence is treated as sufficient to give him value. This occurred at the same time that military service allowed for more personal contact between members of different classes than most had experienced before.

In *Main Street*, worker Miles Bjorstam is one of the most fully portrayed individuals in the book. The cruelty of poverty is shown through Carol Kennicott's eyes as she views the conditions of the slum where Bjorstam lives and the house in which his wife and baby die. Bjorstam's political radicalism is presented as logical because of the conditions shown. He is a rational, intelligent and feeling man.

Other members of the lower economic class also appear more realistically presented than did those before the war. In *If Winter Comes*, a maid Effie, who has an illegitimate baby, is treated as a woman with a problem by hero Mark Sabre. She is a strongly enough defined character to kill herself and the child so Mark won't be blamed for the baby and thus have his life ruined. In *The Bridge of San Luis Rey*, upper class Marquesa de Montemayor and lower class Esteban and Uncle Pio all share the same human fate of craving love and yet being alone, with others' love for them unrealized until after their deaths. The author shows impoverished people reacting just as strongly as anyone else to emotional tragedy.

Partially because of the individualization and partially because of the pursuit of the exotic, differences in values between members of different classes are not nearly so important during this post-war period as they were in the novels that were popular before the war. Where explicit class status is involved, there is most often a question of impoverished but hard-working people seeking to share in the general prosperity or of people trying to share in the exciting living of the rich. The motivation usually is an individual's desire for a certain style of life rather than a drive to be accepted by a higher social class.

The seeking after prosperity is generally done by the individual or for his family. Only a few people like Carol Kennicott in *Main Street* and André-Louis Moreau in *Scaramouche*, a story of the French Revolution, work at least for a while to effect reforms that will better the lot of others generally. More central to their stories are Captain Sorrell of *Sorrell and Son* and Selina Peake DeJong of *So Big* who labor for years so their sons can have an education and a better life in the world. Except for Miles Bjorstam and André-Louis Moreau, most of the feeling is against any class identification in favor of individuality. This is made explicit by Roland, the man who gives Captain Sorrell his chance because he is impressed with him as an individual. Roland complains about the new lower class consciousness:

How I loathe that class—in the mass. We are outside the pale to them. Their sense of honour—such as it is—does not include us. It wasn't always so. . . . We are fair game to most of them. We who have anything, or can do anything a little better than the crowd. We are to be robbed, lied to, blackmailed, slandered. . . . To me it is the individual that matters.[11]

Sorrell, who successfully raises his own status, responds in kind:

. . . the dignity was in the soul of the labourer, not in the matter he worked upon, and a man who cleaned boots with love and care was worthy of the respect of kings.[12]

A third character, Molly Pentreath, who speaks for many of the characters in the novels of the twenties explains her feeling on the matter:

I don't love humanity, and I'm not an improver. God knows—there is enough work in your own job without our making jobs for each other like the Socialists. Nasty people. Want me to pretend with them that I am thinking more of seeing that my neighbors are getting their dinner before I get my own. I'm not. I'm cheerfully and intelligently selfish.[13]

All of these people, like most of the characters in this group of novels are good to the individuals they know, regardless of their class. Yet, of course, such individualism could have been one way of avoiding the whole question of poverty or general responsibility for ameliorating it.

In view of the emphasis on the amusing or emotional rewards of living, it is not surprising that the actual occupation or business of characters was important in very few of the novels. A greater variety of occupations is presented favorably in those of these years than was in the pre-war novels. Farmers and knights, pirates and kings, professors and reporters, as well as doctors and businessmen all caught the popular fancy. Frederick Lewis Allen commented that one of the new elements in post-war society was the attempt by business to justify its conduct.[14] None of this appears in the novels. Nor do businessmen depicted feel the conscious strains of conflict between their role in business and in family and community that have been attributed to them.[15] Sinclair Lewis's *Babbitt* is of course a notable exception to this generalization.

Success is more important than the nature of the occupation, but the success pictured yields rewards in living—in thrills, excitement, goods, and emotional experience—more than in rising to the top of one's profession. During this period, the emphasis the novels placed on both hard work and skill was less than it was in those written before the war. Not surprisingly, hard work is important for its own sake in those books that have the older sort of middle class characters and values. Native skill is important for the same characters and also for those adventurers whose existence depends on it, such men as André-Louis Moreau in *Sacramouche* and Sir Oliver Tressilian in *The Sea Hawk.* The coupling of skill and virtue that was so important before the war has faded. Abstract virtue and personal perfection are no longer prerequisites for either strong ability or a happy life.

Education is also treated differently in the best sellers of the twenties. Formal education no longer lies at the center of a controversy over whether it corrupts natural virtue. In some of the books, education is not a necessity, but it certainly no longer is suspect. Rather, education opens the way up the economic ladder to prosperous living. That is the reason that Selina DeJong in *So Big* and Captain Sorrell work so hard to give their sons good schooling. Education is a tool. The butler Jeeves, in his efforts to improve himself, puts more emphasis on education as an abstract good than do most of the characters in the twenties who treat it as a tool. Jeeves' attitude typifies his embodiment of the old middle class virtues. One of the bases of Jeeves' humor is his old-fashionedness.

Several books place even less importance on formal education. The famous sheik missed out on regular higher education but embodies all sorts of more important masculine strengths. The children of composer Albert Sanger in *The Constant Nymph* grew up in their Alpine home without much schooling but survive and thrive on energy, strength of character, and imagination. So does the blonde who was preferred by so many rich gentlemen despite her bad grammar. During the twenties then, the view of education appears to be split between those who consider it necessary for economic success and those who consider that personal vitality makes it unimportant. These two do not form the basis of any abstract dispute however. The issue obviously was not that important. Either point of view was acceptable.

Art bears roughly the same magnitude of importance during this period as it did in the novels before the war. In some form, art plays a major part in several books and enters into about half the stories in one way or another. No longer however does it represent a pure outpouring of natural goodness or beauty in a soul. Rather it appears to represent a world of excitement, an outlet from everyday routine. This is not to say that the favored art is not honest, but there is no central dispute over the virtues of art for art's sake as opposed to art which is financially remunerative.

An art form was most important in *The Constant Nymph* which revolves around a family of musicians and all the other musicians that come in contact with them. The Sangers and Lewis Dodd who marries one of the Sanger daughters are all escaping English life, which they consider too stratified and too insensitive, through their music and physically by their residence on a Swiss mountain top. The unusual musicality of this family is only one part of the unorthodoxy which give the Sangers their charm.

Art plays a similar although not so all-absorbing function in novels with an American setting. *Main Street* and *The Brimming Cup* show a pattern. In both books, a woman tries to add more art to her life in an effort to alleviate the drabness of small town existence. It is interesting to note that art is often used to add an element of the exotic where there is not a more exotic world of pirates, sheiks, or kings. In these highly adventuresome books, art does not play any important role.

Like art, nature is depicted in these novels without a specific quality of pureness. Characters no longer turn to nature for purification. Nature often is treated as good and natural things as beautiful, but it is to be conquered. It is the nature of the pioneer, not of the conservationist or the man escaping civilization. Zane Grey's man of the forest must give up his woodland solitude and rejoin society. In *The Covered Wagon,* two thousand Americans are travelling into still wild country "taking with them law, order, society, the church, the school. . . ."[16] Untrammelled nature can be threatening. The North African desert is dangerous in *The Sheik* as it is in *Beau Geste.* The sea threatens and takes men's lives in *The Sea Hawk.* Nature is good where it serves mankind and gives satisfaction as it does to Selina DeJong when she makes vegetables grow. It is good when it supports civilization, not when it opposes it. No longer can nature itself be central to a story. It has been reduced to a tool of man. Furthermore, an escape into nature is no longer considered an acceptable substitute for dealing with reality.

This refusal to substitute a rosy haze of nature, belief in purity, or a simplistic life for a recognition of the realities of the world is one of the most important differences between this group of novels and those written before the war. The characters now insist on confronting certain aspects of experience which the pre-war characters avoided.

The authors attempted to analyze society in America and found two elements particularly worthy of condemnation: drabness and conformity. As alternatives to drabness, they put forward exotic places and adventures and art. Conformity is usually attacked through individual non-conformists whose positions are made clear to the readers. The new rejection of conformity involves rejections of the old style middle class life such as Carol Kennicott's, and also rejections of some of the specific thought which was agreed with by most characters before World War I. This again is done in terms of individuals. For example, the decline in racism is shown largely by the refusal to stereotype members of different racial groups. Members of different economic groups receive similar treatment. So also do people whose political philosophies differ from those of the majority of the American people. The authors of the best sellers written during the post-war decade indicate that all these differences—racial, economic and philosophical—do not necessarily make people superior or inferior to each other. Furthermore, there is an assertion that these differences should not be judged or used as a basis for discrimination. This is a significant change from the predominant values expressed in the pre-World War I best sellers when individual differences were considered a valid basis for discrimination.

The most obvious and most significant change from pre-war to post-war popular literature occurred in the area of personal life and morality—home life, the relations between the sexes, and the relationship between the generations. In this realm lies the greatest difference between the attitudes and values expressed in the novels written and read before World War I and those written and read after it. It is more important than the increased cosmopolitanism of the characters and than the change of emphasis from social class to possession of the rewards of money. It is surely connected with the intensification of the values of individualism, *i.e.* the individual's getting out of life what he and he alone considers most satisfying. This individualization of values is reflected in the decline of recommendations of single solutions to all problems: nature as purifier, honesty as cure-all, hard work as the way to success, and so on. The growing individualization of values is, however, most fully expressed in terms of the closest personal relationships.

The family remains a major reference point for characters in most of the books of this period, but the family relationships depicted are no longer mainly those of parents and children. Husband and wife relationships take a predominant position, and in several of the books sibling relationships, usually feuds of one sort or another, play an important role.

Relations between parents and children can be summarized easily. Three basic patterns recur in this group of books. In one pattern, in such books as *Main Street* and *The Brimming Cup,* the children play the passive role as objects of mother love which then has a large part in keeping marriages together. Another is that typified by *So Big* and *Sorrell and Son* where the upbringing of the child is really the life of the parent who spends most of life working to give the child more of a chance. In these books, the children do develop into real people as they grow up, but also end with great respect for their parents. The most typical pattern, however, is one in which the children have serious disagreements with their parents which may or may not be resolved. In *The Private Life of Helen of Troy* there is a dispute over the daughter's proposed husband; in *Scaramouche* it is over political beliefs; in *Elmer Gantry* there is a basic difference of temperament; in *The Bridge of San Luis Rey* it is mistaken pride. In none of these is there an instant reconciliation. The differences are real ones which are not easily solved. Whereas conflicts in the books of the pre-war period were not well defined, here the issues at stake are at least as important as the parent-child relationship itself.

Sibling relationships also are allowed to show hostility. The worst occurs in *The Sea Hawk* where Lionel Tressilian sells his brother Oliver into slavery. Despite a deathbed reconciliation at the end, they hate each other through most of the story. These illustrations indicate a general acknowledgement that family members do not necessarily love each other and live in harmony.

The same is true for husbands and wives. While most of the male-female relationships in the pre-war period stop with young love, married relationships are important in the novels of the twenties. Furthermore, whereas all husbands and wives were on good terms at the end of the books of the earlier period, ten books in this group terminate without a resolution of marital difficulties. Sorrell's wife who left him for richer men while he was a soldier never does return. She is condemned. But divorcée Ellen Olenska in *The Age of Innocence* is not condemned. Nor is married Newland Archer criticized for his love of Ellen. This love continues during his whole life even though he does not terminate his own marriage which he knew in its early years to be a failure:

> . . . with a shiver of foreboding he saw his marriage becoming what most of the other marriages about him were: a dull association of material and social interests held together by ignorance on the one side and hypocrisy on the other.[17]

Marise Crittenden in *The Brimming Cup* makes a positive choice to continue her marriage believing it will give her the most happiness, but Carol Kennicott in *Main Street* slips back into hers which promises no more than a hope of vague contentment. Although heroine Alix Vervier in *The Little French Girl* is destined for marriage, her mother, who is divorced and has affairs, is shown to be a marvelous woman. A contrast is made between Mme. Vervier and the English Mrs. Bradley, whom Alix feels has never been happy because she has always loved more than she received love. A Frenchman explains Mme. Vervier's reward to Giles Bradley: "Mme. Vervier is adored as well as respected."[18] The implication is that wives are not usually adored. In *If Winter Comes,* divorce is shown as a welcome relief in the bad marriage of Mark and Mabel Sabre. Mark is left free to marry the woman he really loves.

By far the most sensational of all marital and extra-marital and also pre-marital relationships are detailed in *The Private Life of Helen of Troy*, which analyzes and satirizes middle class values in the setting of ancient Troy. Helen ran off with Paris and has been brought back by her husband Menelaos. This was not her first or last affair. Menelaos realizes that Helen has always craved a lover who was her equal, and he does not punish her for infidelity because he knows that he has failed to be this man. In another incident, Clytemnestra (Agamemnon's wife) lives with another man, Aegisthus, while Agamemnon is away at the war to retrieve Helen. When he returns, Aegisthus kills Agamemnon. Then Agamemnon's and Clytemnestra's son Orestes kills his mother and Aegisthus. In still another episode, a servant girl Adraste has a child by Damastor, son of pious-talking Charitas, who sends him away to avoid a socially unadvantageous marriage. Helen then takes care of Adraste and the child. Through all of these events, there is a running debate between Helen, who feels that the individual must prevail and that the greatest reward in life is great passion, and her opponents who put society and social convention first. Helen is the one who is kind and who refuses to judge people. She helps when others condemn or gossip. Helen's morality prevails in this book. She is portrayed as neither immoral nor irrational. Rather she acts according to the way she has found life. She comments first on her marriage:

We're not farther apart than most husbands and wives, I dare say, and when we get to the end of our days we'll remember chiefly how long we have been companions.[19]

For her daughter, she hopes for the exceptional: a marriage with real passion, "Two souls melted in that fiery happiness." She says:

It must happen to some people. . . . Those who have it never grow old, I think, never lose courage, nor lose interest; they may suffer, but their world remains beautiful.[20]

Helen blames fate, in the form of people's personalities, but feels that to get what rewards there are, people must accept their fate, accept their personalities, and live as fully as they can:

. . . we come to accept the order of nature, that love can strike again and again, as our personalities develop and change, and our destinies are not so final as we supposed them to be.[21]

Here is the fullest affirmation of individual passion as the basis for living. For modern readers, the Greek setting might suggest that the conclusion is timeless.

Thus infidelity, by women as well as men, and divorce are accepted in a large number of the novels of the twenties. Although some of them still assert the absolute sanctity of marriage, the number that do not make it clear that large numbers of readers were no longer hostile to the more liberal views and freer actions.

Although pre-marital and extra-marital affairs are conducted, there is still little physical description. What does exist, however, is more realistic than what was written before the war. Diana Mayo, when she is travelling around the desert after her sheik has conquered her, longs to be near him physically. In *The Sea Hawk* there is an explicit physical attraction between Oliver and Rosamund. The most detailed physical description occurs in *Elmer Gantry* where Lewis says that Elmer stopped sleeping with his wife after their second child because he was too rough at first and she had never become enthusiastic about making love. The extreme in *Elmer Gantry* is reached when Elmer comments that

Sharon Falconer's lover "must make love like an ice-cream cone."[22] Much more is conveyed through the power of suggestion than through detailed physical description.

Other facets of the relationship between men and women also changed after World War I. Men no longer make up such a large proportion of the central characters. Men are central in thirteen books, women in eight. In the remaining novels they have equally important roles. Nor are men so dominant over women. Men dominate in twelve of the novels, women in nine. Domination does not necessarily correlate with a central position in the novel. The sexes are much more equal in this respect, with neither having a very great degree of dominance over the other. Furthermore, their roles are no longer so clearly differentiated. Although ten of the novels still treat women purely as homebodies, in a larger number of them women are allowed to have jobs or other activities outside the house. And, as was shown above, in many books, women are granted the same sexual freedom as men.

The age of the characters also shows significant changes from the pre-war period. The most important change is the increase in mature adult characters. Whereas young pre-married people and children had such strong roles in the earlier books, mature adults and young people divide the leading roles after the war. This corresponds to the shift away from a simpler, more unified life to the more varied one which involves in so large a degree the search for experience.

Tension between generations does not occur as frequently as it did in the books before the war. It is an element in only half of this group and is not central in most of those. Where stress between the generations does exist, it is in the parent-child relations discussed above. As was noted previously, the stress is on the issues that arouse tension rather than on the specific question of family unity. There is no simple pattern to the solutions of these generational difficulties. The elders dominate twice as often as the younger people do and twice as often as they come out equally, but anybody can win. Furthermore, in some cases there simply is no solution.

Since more older characters play key roles, it is not surprising that the characteristics of growing older are more thoroughly delineated than they were in the earlier period. There is, in fact, more concern with the effects of aging during this period than during any other. Two factors predominate in the conception of age. One is that experience leads to understanding and therefore some form of contentment. The other is that physical decay, a sad thing, accompanies age. The occasions of this range the extremes. Kit Sorrell, a doctor by the end of the book, administers an overdose of morphine to put his father out of his cancerous misery. In *Black Oxen,* 58 year old Marie Zattiany has had chemical treatments on her glands which return physical youth. Physical strength enters more importantly into the books of this period than it does in any other group except the mysteries. When considered along with age, it is generally considered a tragedy that the body must age when experience has shown how to get good things out of life.

Experience is shown to give characters an understanding that makes life more bearable, more complete, or more rewarding. Mme. Zattiany in *Black Oxen* realizes that she must not marry 34 year old Lee Clavering but rather must return to Austria where she can perform an important function as the wife of a political leader. Newland Archer in *The Age of Innocence,* in a less rewarding acceptance, thinks back over his choice not to leave May for Ellen Olenska:

> Something he knew he had missed: the flower of life. But he thought of it now as a thing so unattainable and improbable that to have repined would have been like despairing because one had not drawn the first prize in a lottery.[23]

Although this is a relief for him, the emptiness of his life is presented as a tragedy. The moral, if it can be called that, is live while you have a chance.

Mme. Vervier, in *The Little French Girl,* does live. Despite others' disapproval of her affairs, her experience has taught her what she must do to remain vital. Her daughter Alix's first experience with growing up is hurtful. She has spent an unhappy childhood thinking that her mother did not love her because she was sent away when there were lovers in residence. When Alix first learns about the lovers, she is very hurt. She says:

> Perhaps one only began really to be grown up when one began to know why one was unhappy. A child suffers in ignorance of the cause of its suffering and it can forget more easily because of that merciful vagueness. Unhappiness

is only a cloud to put away or pass out of. But grown-up unhappiness has four solid walls of fact enclosing one.[24]

But Alix passes through this too and, with her increased understanding, is able to achieve real happiness in the end.

As can be seen from Alix's experience, youth is no longer presented as a time of happy innocence as it often was before the war. Nor is there the same kind of envy of youth. Adults, like Marise Crittenden, when she decides not to run away to a world of excitement, rejects a return to the world of youth. Captain Sorrell feels that he has a purpose in life in contrast to his son's lack of purpose at one stage. He comments: "That is youth's trouble. It does not know what it wants."[25] During the twenties, youth is presented as a time of sweet innocence and purity in only those few books that are similar to the pre-war novels and in *When We Were Very Young.* As has already been suggested, the most admired quality of youth is generally its physical strength. The books are full of strong young men: the cowboys, the men of the desert, the pirates, the fighters in the French Revolution.

Most notably, the emphasis has changed from innocence facing the world and youth as a time for education to experience and full living. Some of the youth of the twenties are still innocent and most experience some sort of learning, but the emphasis is no longer there. Instead, the characters show that the wider their range of experience is, the more complete they are as human beings.

From the years before World War I to the years following it, there were great changes in both the appearance and outward behavior of fictional characters in the nation's best sellers. Several things stand out. Characters show a wider variety of age, experience, and background. They are more cosmopolitan. More emphasis is placed on the individual as such rather than as a representative of some group. Family solidarity has declined. Sexual rules have loosened considerably. Most notably, there is a love of and pursuit of adventure, excitement, and deep experience. The question that remains is what sort of beliefs and values underlie the new interests and behavior.

Religion plays a less important role in this group of books than it does in any other. What discussion of religion there is shows greater variety in religious beliefs and practices than did the books before the war. Some Catholics appear in leading roles where there are people from Catholic countries: in *The Four Horsemen of the Apocalypse,* in *The Little French Girl,* and in *The Bridge of San Luis Rey.* More exotically and more heretically, the Allah of the Arabs is accepted not only by the Sheik who is raised with Arabs but also by Oliver Tressilian in *The Sea Hawk* who finds it a convenience when he is captured. Oliver decides in favor of Allah and "that Christianity as practiced in his day was a grim mockery of which the world were better rid."[26] It must be noted, however, that major, non-Protestant characters are all foreign.

Most of the professed Christians emphasize something other than strict orthodoxy. The blonde in *Gentlemen Prefer Blondes* has a very strange version of Christian Science. She explains it:

> Because when something terrible happens to me, I always try to be a Christian science [sic] and I simply do not even think about it, but I deny that it ever happened even if my feet do seem to hurt quite a bit.[27]

There is no prohibition against jesting about religion. Babbitt sees religion socially. He believes that the church is most useful for keeping "the Worst Elements from being still worse."[28] In *Main Street,* atheist Miles Bjorstam is a good man while the religious widow Bogart is nasty. In *The Bridge of San Luis Rey,* religious people who love are good, but many priests are bad. In *The Little French Girl* one of the Protestant characters, Toppie, sees life as just one small stage in the route of souls to heaven. The other characters feel sorry for her because she does not get enough out of life.

Several stunning indictments of Christianity reveal the most deeply felt criticisms of formal religion. In *Elmer Gantry,* Lewis criticizes ministers who are dishonest, who lust after power and financial profit, and who hurt people. In *The Four Horsemen of the Apocalypse,* Tchernoff, a Russian revolutionary, indicts Christianity for placing the promised happiness in heaven. He says:

> . . . my soul is Christian as is that of all revolutionists. The philosophy of modern democracy is lay Christianity. We Socialists love the humble, the needy, the weak.[29]

In both of these, the earthly aspect of religion is emphasized.

Captain Sorrell makes a more personal but at the same time more thorough indictment:

> Sometimes I have felt that there is a plan, but then—there is so much against the idea of a plan. . . . That is the thing that has always got me . . . the fact that there is nothing that cares, the utter-impersonal callousness of the scheme. . . . We don't matter. Man matters only to himself. . . . Man invents religion to hide the full horror of the universe's complete indifference.[30]

Sorrell's disillusion grows out of the hardness of his life. The criticisms of religion in terms of its lack of help in improving human existence appear to be part of the emphasis on life and its experiences that emerges so strongly during the twenties.

The weakening of belief in formal religion is accompanied by a loss of interest in judging the morality or immorality of individuals and their deeds. Human nature is portrayed to range from very good to mildly bad. Some characters change for the better. More do not show any great changes. The goodness and badness of people is not so well defined. There is a more realistic tendency here than there was in the earlier novels to accept people for what they are and let them be that.

During the twenties there are two basic strands of thought on the question of letting people be the individuals they are. Representative of the minority are Sinclair Lewis's books which criticize the forced conformity and show how it injures the individual. A book like *The Age of Innocence* does the same thing in a more sophisticated way. More typical, however, is the book in which conformity simply is not required, in which the assertion of self is made by the leading characters. This is seen in *The Sheik, The Constant Nymph, If Winter Comes* and many others. It seems then that despite the bigotry expressed by some people in the early twenties, the values portrayed in its best sellers suggest that other people were beginning to allow room for differences. Variety, the books indicate, has become interesting. People's horisons are wider.

The acceptance of the variety implies a larger degree of freedom of action. The freedom involved is personal. Political rights and abstract questions of minority rights or economic rights apparently were not interesting to the readers of the twenties. They come to the fore only in terms of individuals. There is less attempt than there was before the war to justify any actions or thoughts by abstract moral principles or generalized creeds. Instead, the central question of the time concerned the meaning of life for the individual, how to live life in the way to give it the deepest emotional and experiential value. The change in emphasis occurs most strongly during the years 1923 to 1925, but it clearly began with the new experiences resulting from the war.

This sort of thought, not flippant but obviously sincere, represents serious consideration of a very serious question. Neither authors nor characters were merely pursuing fun. They were not avoiding seriousness by losing themselves in Mah Jong, speakeasies, and the Charleston. They had not lost their sense of morality. Rather, morality changed its meaning from conforming to general standards to each individual's determining for himself what he wanted in life and going after it. This is the area of greatest rebellion from the values of the pre-war period. Malcolm Cowley used the fact of rebellion to counter the argument of the men who saw the twenties as a time when people gave in to disillusionment. He pointed out that people who are rebelling have faith that they can manage things better than the men in power are doing. This is a position of strength, not of defeat. It is optimism to believe that the world led by men with new standards will be better than that of the old generation.[31] The evidence of the novels supports Cowley's position. Moreover, in one sense at least, their creators surpass even youth in rebellion. The novelists do not attempt to provide the total, easy solution that revolutionaries often think they have found. The only group of best sellers which presented easy solutions appeared from 1914 to 1916. On the other hand, the post-war writers do not make the tragic mistake made by many revolutionaries of believing that all that is needed is total destruction of the contemporary system with no provision for what is to follow. These people have indeed lost their innocence and, during the twenties, they began to exercise their critical powers by analyzing the world they saw and their creative powers by offering varied and sincere suggestions on how to improve life for the individual and the whole society.

The realization of the value of the individual with all his differences in background, actions and desires, is a prerequisite for more generalized toleration and understanding of minority religious and racial groups and for an effective and meaningful concern about victims of economic difficulties. In this sense then, the basis of a really sweeping future change lies in the twenties.

CHAPTER 4

1928-1937: RETREAT TO ABSOLUTISM

Best Selling Novels: 1928-1937

1928	Vina Delmar, *Bad Girl*
1929	Lloyd Douglas, *The Magnificent Obsession*
1929	Erich Maria Remarque, *All Quiet on the Western Front*
1930	Max Brand, *Destry Rides Again*
1930	Edna Ferber, *Cimarron*
1931	Pearl Buck, *The Good Earth*
1933	Hervey Allen, *Anthony Adverse*
1933	Erskine Caldwell, *God's Little Acre*
1933	James Hilton, *Lost Horizon*
1934	James Hilton, *Goodbye, Mr. Chips*
1935	Lloyd Douglas, *Green Light*
1936	W. D. Edmonds, *Drums Along the Mohawk*
1936	Margaret Mitchell, *Gone With the Wind*
1937	A. J. Cronin, *The Citadel*
1937	Kenneth Roberts, *Northwest Passage*

The best selling novels of this group mark the final harkening back to the old values and life style before a change that would be more meaningful in face of the great Depression and the new world situation. The characters in this group of novels show a retreat to the older individualistic values of self-sufficiency, hard work, personal talent, and spirituality. The idea that "where there's a will there's a way" is accepted in many of the stories. It appears that the shock of the severity of the Depression at first inclined many readers to put up defenses against the recognition of the changing order of society. With one exception, these books do not involve group responsibility for the individual's economic well-being. The solutions offered to problems presented are generally spiritual and other-worldly. Some books instead of presenting moral or economic problems provide an escape from all worry.

Despite this negative approach to the Depression, many of the changing directions of the twenties have been retained. Working class people take the role of leading characters more frequently than they did during the previous decade. This continues the trend of bestowing increased dignity on all individuals. Furthermore, the assertion of personal freedom in moral questions is continued and accompanied by an increased earthiness. Sex and other physical descriptions are presented as natural, no longer as something to be hidden.

The gains of the twenties then are largely retained, without the conscious exoticism and necessarily without some of the conscious rebellion in the cases where the rebels had won. The absence of a feeling of economic responsibility may not reflect a retreat by the readers and writers of best sellers but rather a pause before finally coming to grips with reality.

The most important new characteristics are all connected with the solutions to problems that the authors present. Several of the novels contain an overtly expressed spirituality with elements of mysticism or connections with formal religion. These indicate that spiritual strength is all that is needed to make life meaningful and worthwhile. This is one common form of absolutism. Another is the belief that strength of character, determination, is the way to conquer all problems and come out victorious. This is presented as just as absolute a solution as is spiritualism. A number of the books, after the effects of the Depression were being felt, make an attempt to define America and to show the good in the American heritage. This is always coupled with praise of self-sufficiency as the element of character that has made America great. It should be noted that this return to traditional values in the best sellers is very different from the two major forms of more literary works produced during the same time period: the social realism of such men as Steinbeck and Dos Passos and the studies of obsessed men by such authors as Faulkner and Wolfe.

The books in this group number only fifteen. One reason, however, is that twenty-six best-selling mysteries were also written during this period. These form a major part of the Depression escapist literature and will be discussed in the next chapter. All of the books in this group embody one or more of the general characteristics described above. The two books in which the most notable characteristic is the prominent role given to lower class characters are *Bad Girl* and *God's Little Acre*. *All Quiet on the Western Front*, the last of the best sellers about World War I, can also fit into this category because of its concentration on the effects of the war on the common man. Among the books which offer religious value as a solution to the problems faced by their characters are: *The Magnificent Obsession, Green Light*, and *The Citadel*. Other books assert the superior value of traditional attitudes in general, resenting the intrusions of the new ideas of the twenties. *The Good Earth, Lost Horizon*, and *Goodbye, Mr. Chips* fall into this category. Four other books make a traditionalist assertion that American drive and self-reliance can cure all ills. These are: *Destry Rides Again, Cimarron, Drums Along the Mohawk*, and *Northwest Passage*. It should be noted further that the representation of lower class heroes and the reassertion of the preeminence of spiritual values began before the Depression, but that the emphasis on the value of hard work as well as the most severe escapism appeared after the effects of the Depression were being felt.

Two books remain. These are the two historical epics written during this period: *Anthony Adverse* and *Gone With the Wind*. The plots of both take place in an America of the past and both show that hard work can bring success. Both also allow a certain escape from current reality because their length permits long-term identification with a different era by the readers.

Despite the general conservatism of the authors, they represent a varied group. They range in age from twenty-three to fifty-six years, making the range younger than that of the authors of the twenties. These writers were born between 1877 and 1905, from eight to twenty years later than the authors of the previous period. Any conservatism therefore is not a factor of older age. The authors come from a varied geographical background: four from the Northeast, two from the Middle West, one from the West, four from the South, and five from foreign countries. The most noteworthy changes are the decline in representatives of the Middle West and foreign countries and the increase in Southerners.

As was already mentioned, longer books came into vogue during this period as did historical novels. Six of the fifteen books must be classified as historical novels, all of which deal at least partially with earlier days in America. Despite the interest in America, in over half the novels at least part of the action takes place on foreign soil. This represents no great change from the cosmopolitanism of the twenties. Of the regions in America, the Northeast is a locale in four books, the Middle West and the West in three each, and the South in two. In one-third of the books, at least some of the action takes place in a large city and in smaller cities in several more. But towns, various sorts of farms and ranches, and undeveloped areas all receive a similar portion of the treatment. The great change from the early and middle twenties is the lack of the exotic element. With the exception of *Lost Horizon* none of the books involve such improbable situations as Englishmen on pirate ships or English women as captive in the North African desert.

There are several changes in style from the preceding period. A higher proportion of the books are written in less sophisticated, more straightforward English and in this way bear a greater resemblance to those of the pre-World War I period than to those of the twenties. Use of colloquial language and foreign words or phrases is reduced only slightly from the novels of the twenties. One notable increase is in the use of regional and class dialects. The latter appear in over one-third of the books. This may represent a part of the pattern of exploring different phases of American history and life.

During this period, despite the prevalence of escape through other means, humor is considerably reduced in importance. It bears only moderate importance in four of the novels. Where humor does occur, family life and day-to-day events are the basis of most of it. This resembles the humor before the war. Attacks on accepted values or authorities still provide some humor, but not as much as they did during the twenties. The same is true of humor at the expense of individual characters. The big increase is in ethnic humor, a point that is developed later in the chapter.

The most notable change in style corresponds with the more general change in emphasis in this group of novels. Whereas the best sellers of the twenties often presented serious problems in comic style, the novels of the thirties employ a more serious tone. The great energy and lively zest for adventure and amusement that was so strong, particularly in the mid-twenties, was missing already by the late twenties. This new group of novels, unlike the earlier one, contains many serious discussions of abstract issues rather than presenting these in terms of an individual person in a given situation.

The primary reaction of the best selling novelists of this decade to both the international and domestic political, social and economic crises taking place was to bury their heads and ignore them even more than they did in earlier periods. They were not unaware of them, of course, but for the most part they expressed their dislike of what was happening by withdrawing to a world which was safe and familiar. Generally, the authors do not specifically mention the political innovations of the New Deal. Instead, they express their disapproval by asserting an opposing set of values.

Politics received little attention during the twenties, but that was an age of political drabness. The best sellers of the thirties give it little more attention despite the fact that this was an era of international crisis and domestic governmental innovation. International political concerns receive almost no attention whatever. What slight comments there are indicate a deep distrust of the whole international system. There is a general loss of faith in the world's political leaders and their motivations. Erich Maria Remarque in *All Quiet on the Western Front* condemns all the concerned governments and their leaders for causing the war of which not they but the common soldiers must suffer the consequences. James Hilton's hero Conway in *Lost Horizon* has been a diplomat but is led by the horrors of war to seek a passive and peaceful life. Rather than try to work through the channels of diplomacy to create a better world, he prefers non-involvement. Another character in *Lost Horizon* apparently despairs of the chance that the world's leaders will succeed in creating a good society. This is Father Perrault who has built the Himalayan

Shangri-La in the hope that it will survive when the rest of the world is destroyed. In Kenneth Roberts' *Northwest Passage,* one of the historical novels treating early America, the hero Langdon Towne, whose work brings him in contact with leading American and British politicians, judges them to be evil men:

I knew that no villain upon the stage can equal, in brutal and malignant rascality, many of those honored gentlemen who, by ruthlessness and sharp practice, have achieved the highest offices and are bent on holding them.[1]

The disillusionment with traditional international political processes is much more strongly expressed here than it was during the twenties. Furthermore, there is no recommendation for improvement of the system, only resignation from it. And there is no leaning towards involvement where it might do some good in the contemporary situation. Not one of the authors deals with the developments in Europe. None expresses concern with Hitler or with fascism.

Domestic politics are viewed with more tolerance than are contemporary international practices. In several books there is some criticism of corruption: in *Northwest Passage* and in *Cimarron* where Yancey Cravat refuses to run for office, describing it as:

Palavering to a lot of greasy office seekers and panhandlers! Dancing to the tune of that gang in Washington! I know the whole dirty lot of them.[2]

But his wife Sabra Cravat acquires an interest in politics and, believing it a useful way to accomplish desirable ends, goes to Congress and does achieve some good. In both Margaret Mitchell's *Gone With the Wind* and Hervey Allen's *Anthony Adverse,* the characters become involved in politics as a means to their own ends. There is no particular definition of good or bad. The reader rather is encouraged to identify with the desires of Scarlett O'Hara and Anthony Adverse in their pursuit of success.

In several of the novels, politics plays an even less important role and receives very off-hand treatment. James Hilton in *Goodbye, Mr. Chips* creates a suffragette whose political activism is mildly comical. In Vina Delmar's *Bad Girl*, political ignorance is accepted happily. A young New York City lower class couple discusses the 1928 election. Dot Collins says that she likes Al Smith because he is a New Yorker like herself. Her husband Eddie says that Smith "won't do" because he is a Catholic. He adds: "Don't know much about it, but that's what the boss says."[3] This attitude is accepted as natural. Clearly these novels are for the most part apolitical.

Surprisingly enough, the only constructive attitude towards government appears in the escapist *Lost Horizon.* James Hilton describes the government Conway comes to see as somewhat utopian in Shangri-La:

> Conway was puzzled as to the ultimate basis of law and order; there appeared to be neither soldiers nor police, yet surely some provision must be made for the incorrigible? Chang replied that crime was very rare, partly because only serious things were considered crimes, and partly because everyone enjoyed a sufficiency of everything he could reasonably desire.[4]

This idea that sufficiency of goods is a prerequisite for stability is the only sign of agreement any of these novels seem to have with New Deal type government. Clearly there is no concern for the realities of government and governing.

Richard Hofstadter says that the Depression led to a demand for reform and that the New Deal reformers upheld practical realities rather than abstract ideals.[5] These tendencies are not reflected in the novels. The indication is that perhaps the middle and upper class readers of best sellers were out of step with or escaping from politicians, reformers, and the masses who were more personally affected by the Depression. Several of the novels present a very conservative, anti-welfare position, asserting the old American idea of self-reliance. When Anthony Adverse arrives in New Orleans, which is still French, he becomes friends with many men, judged good, who are refugee Tories from the American Revolution. They openly express their disillusionment with the results of the Revolution saying that there has been too much equalization while the talents of men are not equal.

In 1936 in *Drums Along the Mohawk,* Walter Edmond's novel about people of the Mohawk Valley who fight in the American Revolution despite the lack of aid from the Eastern-biased Continental Congress, an only thinly veiled comment on the New Deal is made:

> Those people of the valley were confronted by a reckless Congress and ebullient finance, with the inevitable repercussions of poverty and practical

starvation. The steps followed with automatic regularity. The applications for relief, the failure of relief, and then the final realization that a man must stand up to live. . . . Finally, though they had lost two-thirds of their fighting strength, these people took hold of their courage and struck out for themselves.[6]

The predominant political tone then tends to be either apathetic or critical of the sort of policies instituted under Franklin Roosevelt. The popularity of these books may reflect a failure of their readers to accept the New Deal. Parrington's assertion that careless individualism holds sway over real democracy still appears to be true for the group whose values are represented in these books.[7]

This failure by some writers and readers to accept the New Deal does not reflect a lack of concern for America or a lack of consciousness that something profound was happening to the country. There is, in fact, a strong search for a definition of what America is and means. Daniel Boorstin's idea that the belief in the existence of an American theory has made such theory unnecessary does not hold true for this period.[8] During the Depression, many of the authors very consciously spelled out their definition of America. This takes two basic forms. The first is portraiture of the different regions of the country which carries the implication that all the variations are part of a common heritage which should be appreciated by all. *Gone With the Wind* is a book about the old, upper-class South. *God's Little Acre* describes the newly recognized poorer South. *Bad Girl* is about life of lower class people in New York City. *Destry Rides Again* is about the old pioneer West. *Cimarron* begins in the old West but emerges into the modern age of accumulated wealth. This portrayal of the wide variety of American life is in greatest contrast to the pre-war books from which the reader might have concluded that all Americans lived in middle class towns or suburbs of the East or Middle West.

The other sort of definition of America is the fictional recreation of its past. A higher percentage of historical novels of America sold during this period than during any other in this study. The pioneers, the plantation people of the early South and, most strongly, the residents of the colonies around the time of the American Revolution are all heroes. The one trait they share in common from *Cimarron* to *Gone With the Wind* to *Northwest*

Passage and *Drums Along the Mohawk* is a capacity for hard work which always results in success. This appears to be a search for historical justification of the anti-New Deal position. But there may be more than that. There may be a seeking after reassurance that the old belief in self-reliance is still a valid basis for a political system. American history is used for comfort before a final recognition that the world was indeed different. This use of history may be a backward attempt at assertion of basic American goodness and strength while refusing to face the necessity for political change. Given this apparent reactionary attitude of the readers of best sellers towards government, it seems most appropriate to investigate what happened to the conscious acceptance of individual men that grew during the twenties. This recognition of individual worth can be considered as a prerequisite for valid reform. Ethnic perceptions will be treated first, then class divisions.

Despite the racism of European fascists and despite the poverty of the Depression which affected certain ethnic groups more severely than others, this group of readers showed little interest in race or problems arising from racial differences. Race is of moderate importance in six of the fifteen novels but in none is it a primary theme. In an overwhelming majority of the books, all the important characters are white, Anglo-Saxon Protestants. Other racial types are not brought in or appear only in a very minor way.

Negroes receive more treatment than any other racial group. The most favorable comment comes, not surprisingly, from a book of the late twenties, *Bad Girl.* Dot Haley sees Negro patients in the sanitarium where she has gone to have her baby. At first she is taken aback:

> "Gee," thought Dot. "Niggers. But I guess you don't care who your neighbors are once the pain starts."[9]

This is the attitude of the twenties.

In all the later books in this group, the attitude most favorable to Negroes is paternalistic. In *Cimarron,* Sabre Cravat loves and takes care of a Negro servant boy named Isaiah. His chief function in the book is providing comic relief by behaving in a slightly subhuman manner. In both *Anthony Adverse* and *Gone With the Wind,* the slave system is accepted. Although Anthony believes that the system is bound to end someday, he acts in what he judges a moral fashion by being paternalistic to his slaves. In *Gone With the Wind,* the only good Negroes are the ones like Mammy who are loyal and obedient to their white masters. Although the close proximity of living is shown (slave Dilcey nurses Melanie's baby) the Negroes are portrayed as incapable of taking care of themselves in freedom.

The only meaningful presentation of Negro life comes in 1933 in Erskine Caldwell's book *God's Little Acre.* Two Negroes live on the farm of Southern poor white Ty Ty Walden. Like the slave characters, they cannot care for themselves very well. They often go hungry when Ty Ty does not have enough to feed them. They are ignorant and superstitious. But they are at least proud that they do not have the disease which some of the whites have. Notably, their plight is presented less seriously by Caldwell than is that of the poor whites. However, from his presentation, it is obvious that the economic welfare of the two groups is tied together.

In all of the books Negroes speak a dialect that is written out with mispronunciations and bad grammar. In most they are referred to as Niggers. Negroes are most de-humanized in Max Brand's Western, *Destry Rides Again.* Mr. Dangerfield, a ranch owner, jests with his daughter about the poor quality of the corn bread:

> I'm gunna kill me a nigger out yonder in the kitchen one of these days, if you don't bring 'em to time pretty quick![10]

Even though he probably wouldn't kill a Negro for cornbread, he obviously does not consider a Negro's life to have the same value that a white man's does. He comments further on the general question of what is to become of Negroes. "Money and votes ain't no good for them."[11] Although Dangerfield is not the most important character in the book, nobody disputes his views.

In *Drums Along the Mohawk,* Negroes are portrayed as silly and incompetent. One slave woman gets pregnant. When asked who the father is, she says:

> I guess hit's from that Hans of Mr. Grebb's. . . . He de pesteringest nigger. I jus' couldn' think of no other way to get rid of him.[12]

This speech is typical of that attributed to Negro characters.

In the best sellers, Negroes have lost rather than gained status from the twenties to this period. The change in attitudes follows the onset of the Depression and its accompanying fears and rivalries. There is no more assertion that Negroes are individuals like white men. And the situation is only slightly better for several other minority groups.

American Indians receive a fair amount of attention because of the number of books set in the early West. Langdon Towne, the hero of *Northwest Passage* likes some Indians but generalizes that "most of them are simple to absurdity."[13] In *Drums Along the Mohawk,* although some Indians can be good and some even educated, they are most noticeably dirty and smelly. The author of this book does accept the fact that illegitimate half-breed offspring, even of high-born whites, are living among the Indians. Only in *Cimarron* do the characters come to respect the Indians and fight for their rights.

Jews receive better treatment than Negroes or Indians, but they are still singled out and stereotyped. In *Bad Girl,* Eddie Haley expressed a lower class view of Jews which the author accepts as a natural one for lower class New Yorkers. When he meets a Jewish doctor, Eddie comments:

> This fellow's a Jew. . . . When they ain't the common, money-grabbing kind, they're kind of erratic.[14]

Several of the books contain Jewish businessmen who are shown to be good men but different. Sol Levy in *Cimarron* always holds himself aloof from the social life of the other characters. Perhaps because of this, he is accepted in the high business councils of Osage where the story is set. In *Northwest Passage,* there is a similar separated stereotype. Ezekiel Solomon is also portrayed as a nice guy, but he has "the business energy of his race."[15]

Anthony Adverse is the only book in which any effort is made to fight stereotyping and, even here, Jews are still merchants and bankers, but so are Gentiles. Anthony meets a man named Mayer, a future Rothschild. They become friends when Anthony treats him as if he does not expect him to be greedy. Mayer comments on this:

> You are the first Gentile I ever met who did not imagine that because I am a Jew I am also Shylock. That play I am sure has cost Christendom infinite millions.[16]

This is the only assertion that stereotyping is wrong to occur in any of the books in this group.

Interestingly enough, the only racial group that receives a favorable presentation is Orientals living, not in America, but in the Far East. Two novels have Oriental characters. In *Lost Horizon*, there are Chinese monks in the lamasery in Shangri-La. It should be noted, however, that the leaders of the lamasery are all Westerners. In this book only the hero, Conway, regards the Chinese as equals rather than inferiors. He argues the point with the others that have come with him, but neither side convinces the other. A fuller picture of Chinese life is given in Pearl Buck's novel about the family of Wang Lung, *The Good Earth*. Love of the land, hard work, steadiness and loyalty to family, not the exoticism of the Orient, are the qualities that Pearl Buck considers superior in these people.

Despite the comparatively favorable presentation of Far Easterners residing in the East, it is fairly obvious that during the period of Depression, the characters expressed only little concern for and a fairly general dislike of minority racial groups living in this country. In fact, the attitude towards minorities is less tolerant than it was during the twenties. Negroes are portrayed as extremely inferior, as are most Indians. Jews, while not necessarily bad, are outcasts. Southern and Eastern European immigrant groups are not considered at all. During the twenties, there was no sense of responsibility, nor is there here. But now there is more antagonism than there was in the previous decade. This would appear to be the reaction to the threat contained in the poor economic conditions and the resultant New Deal. Minorities and their protectors perhaps are seen more as competition and therefore the object of antagonistic feelings than they were during more prosperous times. The easy toleration of the sunny days seems to have disappeared among this middle class group that possibly felt the New Deal policies would take away from them to give to the others. One group of Americans, at least, is not living up to the first part of Myrdal's American creed: "the ideals of the essential dignity of the individual human being, of the fundamental equality of all men."[17] Economic fear may have taken precedence over these ideals.

The idea that racial attitudes have an economic basis can be supported by the way the authors handle the relations among the fictional characters of different classes. Lower class characters have fewer friendly relationships with middle and upper class ones. It would have been possible to have more examples of such relationships because of the greater presentation of realistically portrayed lower class people. Lower class characters are prominent in nearly one-third of this group of novels, a 300% increase over the preceding period. Eddie Collins, hero in *Bad Girl*, is a radio repairman. The soldiers in *All Quiet on the Western Front* come mainly from the working classes. Wang Lung and his family in *The Good Earth* begin as peasants and pass through a period of crop failure when they must beg for food before he becomes a big landowner. The family of Ty Ty Walden in *God's Little Acre* remain poor farmers throughout.

The conflict between classes is more pronounced in *All Quiet on the Western Front.* Remarque points out several times that the souls of the common men are being destroyed because of decisions of upper class leaders of the government. He repeatedly asserts that the German and French soldiers have no quarrel, that both are being victimized by their upper class rulers who alone benefit from the war. In *The Good Earth* the conflict between rich and poor is implied when the author shows the effects of poverty on individuals. People are forced to beg and even steal to prevent starvation. The rulers obviously exploit the poor, as do the sons of Wang Lung when they finally become rich. In these three books the source of and justification for possible conflict is shown much more than the conflict itself.

Class conflict is most explicit in *God's Little Acre.* After Jim Leslie has moved away from the farm and into town where he has a steady job and therefore more money than Ty Ty Walden and his family, Jim becomes a snob and wants nothing more to do with the country people. This hurts Ty Ty and the others. Conflict has even more tragic results when Will Thompson, husband of one of Ty Ty's daughters, leads a strike against the mill owners who are portrayed as evil. Will, the strong hero, is slain and with him the hope of the workers for a decent wage. Before he is killed, Will makes a forthright statement of the humanity of lower class people:

> Back there in Georgia, out there in the middle of all those damn holes and piles of dirt, you think I'm nothing but a dead sapling sticking up in the ground. Well, maybe I am over there, But over here in the Valley, I'm Will Thompson. You come over here and look at me in this yellow company house and you think that I'm nothing but a piece of company property. And you're wrong about that, too. I'm Will Thompson. I'm strong as God Almighty Himself now, and I can show you how strong I am. Just wait till tomorrow morning and walk down the street there and stand in front of the mill. I'm going up to that door and rip it to pieces just like it was a window shade. You'll see how strong I am.[18]

This is a new kind of language spoken by a new kind of character. Although Will dies, the reader is supposed to be fighting along with him against the evil owner.

God's Little Acre also makes the strongest demonstration of the effects of poverty on the poor. These farmers are too ignorant to know how to make their land yield much. Poverty leads at least some of them to unproductive dreaming which not only wastes time but can be really destructive as it is when Ty Ty digs up his farm looking for gold. Furthermore, the poverty forms the basis of much personal tragedy. Because they are ignorant and because they have so little money for diversions, sex is their main outlet. This leads to competition among brothers and brothers-in-law for the same woman ending in hatred and death. Still, what is surprising is not the inclusion of *God's Little Acre* on the list of best sellers but the lack of other books like it. The sales record of *God's Little Acre* indicates a beginning recognition or perhaps the beginning of an education of the readers, but its uniqueness also gives a measure of the lack of concern by the reasonably well off for those who are less fortunate.

The more strongly expressed economic concern is with the problems faced by the middle class itself. This group was hurt but not driven to near starvation by the Depression. There are several different reactions expressed. The first is the re-assertion of the ideals of hard work and self-sufficiency. This is often presented together with praise of America. The second is a reaction against possession of too much money and against the very rich. In *Drums Along the Mohawk,* the heroes are the middle class farmers of the

Mohawk Valley. They consider the Yankees, i.e. the men on the coast whom they imagine to be rich, almost as much their enemy as the British. The Yankees are portrayed as rich snobs who have no concern for the life or well-being of the farmers who fight so hard in the battle for independence. Edmonds presents the farmers as clearly superior. They are more self-sufficient, braver, and more democratic. Even in the novel of the Old South, *Gone With the Wind,* the members of the old plantation aristocracy, such as Ashley Wilkes, who never learn to do anything except be genteel, lose their dominant position to people like Rhett and Scarlett who can make their own prosperity. This book, however, most closely resembles the novels of the twenties in its economic view: money is more important than social status.

In most books the challenge to the monied aristocracy comes in another form. This is the spiritual protest against emphasis on both money and social status. This is strongest in Lloyd Douglas's books. For example, in *Green Light*, Dr. Endicott makes errors in an operation and kills a patient because he is so upset about the stock market crash. He is solidly condemned for allowing his concern for money to outweigh that for a human life. Another doctor, Andrew Manson in *The Citadel,* is condemned when he tries to get into London society by treating rich patients with imaginary illnesses and loses interest in the patients who really need him. Even in *Anthony Adverse*, which deals with the business world and its people during the eighteenth century, money is never more important than emotions for the good characters. In all of this then is an indication that the Depression might have led some people to assert that money really was not so important after all.

The occupations of the leading characters reflect the emphasis on the spiritual and the simple life as opposed to the materialistic or society life. Eight of the fifteen books are about doctors or farmers. Of slightly less importance are ministers, artists, soldiers and government employees. The only well delineated capitalists are Anthony Adverse and Rhett Butler. In five of the books, businessmen are the villains as are the idle or rich playboys in three more. These villains include the carpetbagging businessmen in *Gone With the Wind,* the playboy Freddie Hampton in *The Citadel,* and the mill owner in *God's Little Acre.* This pattern marks a notable contrast to the twenties when the rich were often the heroes because their money enabled them to lead exciting lives.

Furthermore, the kind of occupation and the achievement of success at accepted ones (medicine, farming, the ministry, pioneering) are judged much more important than they were in either of the earlier periods. The type of occupation finally chosen by a man and how he performs in this are of major importance in two-thirds of the books of this group. Work for its own sake is not of as much importance as the nature of the work.

Even so, people work harder in this group of books than they do in any other. In *Magnificent Obsession* Robert Merrick studies very diligently to become a good brain surgeon. In *Cimarron* Sabra Cravat strives to create a good newspaper and then to keep it going. Anthony Adverse works hard to achieve the financial success he finally does. In *Drums Along the Mohawk* Gil Martin works first to get a farm and then to keep it prospering. In *Gone With the Wind* Scarlett works almost desperately to get money to rebuild Tara. The capacity for work thus is shared by those few characters who do actively pursue wealth and also by those who want to achieve greatness or who want merely a decent life for their families.

In the best sellers of all the periods innate skill is considered of more importance than work. Skill in doctoring, skill in farming, skill in dealing with people—whatever the kind of skill—is extremely important. It is almost required that the hero be skilled in whatever he has chosen to do. This view of skill, which could also be called cleverness, intelligence and so on, would be flattering to the middle and upper class readers who could then assume that they, like the heroes, must be skilled, as they were fairly successful.

Skill supercedes not only work but also education as the crucial factor in success. But education is considered important. Education is often a prerequisite for the careers of the heroes. The doctors, especially, are shown to be good students. Education during this period is primarily a way to acquire the training necessary for success at a specific occupation. There is no accusation against education as being unnatural as there was before World War I, nor is there any exotic substitution for education as there was during the twenties. Education is rarely the subject of abstract discussion. Instead, it is a tool. *Goodbye, Mr. Chips* is, of course, the exception to that generalization. In this book there is a debate between Mr. Chips, a teacher who considers his primary job to be character building and a new headmaster Ralston who proposes newer, more scientific methods for imparting knowledge. Chips wins out in the minds of the author and readers. He is like the characters of Lloyd Douglas who put morality before any more material or practical aspect of life. Even for Mr. Chips, education is his tool for imparting morality. On the other hand, it is during this period that the largest portion of authors indicate specifically that education is not needed for successful living. The three books about pioneers, *Destry Rides Again, Drums Along the Mohawk,* and *Northwest Passage,* all share this point of view.

Unlike the periods from 1914 to 1916 and 1918 to 1927, art is largely ignored in the best sellers of 1928 to 1937. The emphasis on economic conditions and spiritualism and Americana allow little room for such a diversion. Only in *Lost Horizon* does it play any significant role. Conway, the leader of the group of outsiders in Shangri-La finds Chinese art a peaceful change from all the turbulence of the modern world. "His liking for Chinese art was an affair of the mind; in a world of increasing noise and hugeness, he turned in private to gentle, precise, and miniature things."[19] Since this exotic sort of escapism was alien to most of the authors, no others gave art this kind of treatment. Mostly, escapism gave way to practicality in material pursuits or assertion of spiritual values as the cure for life's problems.

Like art, the role of nature has also declined in importance. It plays a major role only in *The Good Earth* where the Chinese farmer's love of the land is so strong, where the land produces at man's bidding, nature is judged good. It is never used as an escape from human problems as it was in the pre-war period. The most significant aspect of the presentation of nature is that it is judged threatening to civilization more during this period than during any other. It is as if the economic insecurity gave rise to insecurity in other areas. In *Cimarron,* Sabra Cravat works hard to overcome natural obstacles to recreating Eastern life in the early West. In *God's Little Acre, Drums Along the Mohawk,* and *Northwest Passage,* characters must fight the elements to survive. Nature, like art, is no longer an agent of salvation. As Henry Steele Commager pointed out, Americans in the twentieth century were losing contact with nature.[20]

In general, then, the attitude towards the outside world expressed in the best sellers of the Depression reveals a turning away from more general concerns in favor of more personal ones. The international political system is rejected when it is shown to have damaging effects on individual lives. More importantly, the middle and upper class readers fail to care about most things not immediately in their own benefit. This is illustrated by the lack of concern for the poor and for ethnic minorities and by the rejection of the philosophy of the New Deal. Basically, during this period, the books are concerned with the problems of the middle and upper-middle class in Depression America. Two primary reactions to those economic conditions are expressed. One is the re-assertion that the old values of hard work and self-reliance will and *ought to* bring a man out on top. The second is that a man should seek spiritual and other than material comfort. All of this adds up to an unwillingness to recognize the changes in and desperate needs of the society outside the readers' own immediate group. The novels seem to indicate that this decade was a period of shock before a final acceptance of reality.

The greatest change following World War I lay in the area of personal relations. Families were shown to be less harmonious and the codes of sexual behavior loosened considerably. The same pattern continued to exist in the best sellers of 1928 to 1937, with little further development. Relationships among adults again predominate. Most often these are between husband and wife. Many married people have affairs or, for a while at least, love someone other than their spouse. Most of these are men during this period. Yancey Cravat in *Cimarron* periodically deserts his wife. Wang Lung in *The Good Earth* takes two mistresses, one to demonstrate his newly acquired prosperity and one young girl in his old age. Andrew Manson in *The Citadel* has a brief affair with rich and glamorous Frances Lovejoy. Of the women, Scarlett O'Hara is long unfaithful to her husbands in thought but never has the chance to put the thought into action. Numerous characters both male and female in *God's Little Acre* are unfaithful. There the idea of animal instinct in humans is very important. These examples, by no means all, show that there was not a return to the pre-war ideals of purity and family solidarity. Yet something from the twenties is missing. That is the consciousness of daring and excitement when family relations are anything other than well regulated. Unfaithfulness is no longer a daring action about which the whole plot revolves. This fact is particularly true for two reasons.

The first reason is that women no longer appear to be rebelling against playing a secondary role in society. Describing Florence Adverse, wife of Anthony, Hervey Allen writes:

> Nor was Mrs. Adverse worried about her position as a woman. She had no doubt of it. Nor did she, when the baby proved to be a girl, try to call it by a boy's name. She acquiesced with the universe in the difference, and in a name which admitted it. Poor woman, her status was too secure and her life too full for her even to have thought of signing herself by her father's name after she was married in order to prove that she was independent of the conventions of men.[21]

Allen is obviously defending his own idea of what women should be, but a large number of readers apparently agreed with his rejection of the modernism of the previous decade.

The second difference is that during the twenties unfaithfulness was one method of rebellion. This is no longer so important. The question then is what role do they play. And the answer is that they become just one part of family relations which are also less important here than they were previously. The individual, his own achievements and happiness, is more important than the individual as part of a family. In *The Citadel,* Manson's way of going about his work is emphasized more than his relations with his wife. In *Cimarron,* the ability of each character to find and achieve some satisfaction in work is always at least equal in importance to the love story. In *Goodbye, Mr. Chips,* a book which has nothing to do with sex, Chips' marriage plays a very secondary role compared to his teaching. Family thus has developed from a sacred institution to an institutional object of rebellion to something that is just a given circumstance, one that is different in each individual case.

Accompanying the decreased excitement over family irregularities is an increase in the volume of and detail in descriptions of sexual activities. Here is the only possible new area of sensationalism in the novels of the Depression period. *The Good Earth, God's Little Acre, Anthony Adverse* and *Bad Girl* all have their share of more vivid physical description than was used in the twenties. Connected to this is the more open discussion of topics that were never really treated before. *Bad Girl* contains a discussion of abortion. Although Dot decides not to have one, all the details of how, including the price, are put in print.

A passage spoken by Ty Ty Walden in *God's Little Acre* illustrates not only how openly such things as extra-marital relations are being discussed but also how the emphasis has changed from emotional excitement to the physical:

> There was a mean trick played on us somewhere. God put us in the bodies of animals and tried to make us act like people. . . . If He had made us like we are, and not called us people, the last one of us would know how to live. A man can't live, feeling himself from the inside and listening to what the preachers say. He can't do both, but he can do one or the other. He can live like we were made to live, and feel himself on the inside, or he can live like the preachers say, and be dead on the inside. . . . The girls understand, and they are willing to live like God made them to live; but the boys go off and hear fools talk and they come back here and try to run things counter to God. God made pretty girls and He made men, and there was enough to go around. When you try to take a woman or a man and hold him off all for yourself, there ain't going to be nothing but trouble and sorrow the rest of your days.[22]

This kind of material is not, of course, included in all the books of this group, but that does not detract from the fact that this is much more blunt than anything written during the twenties. Also different is the fact that Ty Ty is not being consciously daring in saying this. He is speaking his honest thoughts. The rebellion of the twenties has been accepted in deed. Attention has now turned to the causes and effects of the deeds. Furthermore, these are viewed in a complex manner. The hurt to individuals in a family because of a lack of family solidarity or matrimonial loyalty is shown, but the cause is also shown and understood just as deeply.

Husbands and wives thus have a varied relationship in the novels of the thirties. Some get along well, and some fight. Some are faithful, and some are not. Some who disagree are reconciled at the end of the story, and some are not. This variety is more realistic than were the innovations of the twenties which sometimes were stylized to meet the demands of conscious rebellion or because it was a new thing to discuss then and therefore writers were more self-conscious about it.

One further significant aspect of the relations between men and women is the fact that men regain their position of dominance which had declined in strength in the novels of the post-war decade. As in the pre-war books, men are predominantly the central characters. Only in *Bad Girl* does a woman play a role more important than any man. Furthermore, the men are dominant over their women. Most of the extra-marital sex during this period is by the men. There is a tendency to return to differentiating between the sexes in the realms of both thought and action. It is interesting that the primary loss of strength among male characters occurred during a decade of prosperity and immediately following a period when men functioned as warriors. They regained their strength in the best selling novels of a period when there was no war and when economic depression made many of them less powerful breadwinners.

Just as there is a variety of relations between men and women, husbands and wives, there is also variety in the relations between children and parents, between the young and the old. More of the leading characters are young married people or young unmarried adults than any other age group. But all groups from children to the aged are represented. A far greater percentage of these books trace a whole generation or more than do books in any other period. These are: *Cimarron, The Good Earth, Anthony Adverse* and *Gone With the Wind.* In all of them, the characters remain fairly constant as they grow older. Age does not bring great changes in personality or morality. Young people can be wiser than their parents as in Dot Haley in *Bad Girl* or Cim in *Cimarron.* On the other hand, young people are sometimes portrayed as foolish or evil because of their failure to espouse their parents' values. The greedy sons in *The Good Earth* are one such example. Sometimes older people understand and help members of the younger generation as does Mrs. McKlennar in *Drums Along the Mohawk* or John Bonnyfeather in *Anthony Adverse.* In at least one case the older generation is blamed for harming the younger. This occurs in *All Quiet on the Western Front,* because it caused the war that hurt the young soldiers so greatly. In all of this mixture of traits, two portrayals of age dominate all others: age as a time of wisdom and understanding and age as a time of physical decay. Just as there are vivid descriptions of the physical elements of sex, there are also fairly detailed accounts of the physical elements of aging and dying. All these things are treated as natural physical processes and described with a similar earthiness.

Youth, on the other hand, is not presented as carrying any specific general characteristic. A few young people are objects of instruction and a few rebel. Mostly, they just live life as it comes to them, as individuals rather than members of a generation. Many of the books include some tension between younger and older people, but it is central only in *The Good Earth* where the sons lose all the moral values of their father in their over-emphasis on wealth and what it can buy.

There is thus, during this period, a settling down of relations between the generations and the sexes. The generalized rebellions of the twenties have disappeared and are replaced by more individualized conflicts and by a slight increase in harmony. This may be a secondary result of the emphasis on success and moral living in the wider world and the corresponding broadening of the base of important relationships. Since people are no longer searching so much for new values there is not the automatic necessity for friction with what already exists. Furthermore, because of the acceptance during the twenties of many new freedoms–sexual liberalization, women's rights, etc.–the need for such strong assertion of new ideas has declined and therefore also the hostility that normally accompanies the change.

Since rebellion, the search for meaning, and the emphasis on living life fully have declined in importance, one most look elsewhere for the main values underlying the conduct of the characters of the best sellers of this period. The post-war period had marked a turning away from religion and spiritual belief. The rebellion over, the thirties shows a return to religious belief and spiritualism. The religion is less of God than of man. Like the period before the war, this period also emphasizes the spiritual basis of man's treatment of man. And the recommendation is love. Perhaps this is a delayed reaction to the war–love as an antidote to the evils which cause wars and suffering. Perhaps it reflects a feeling of helplessness against the economic problems of the Depression and therefore represents a search for a place to hide. Probably it is some of each since the renewed search for religion began before the onset of the Depression in such books as *The Bridge of San Luis Rey*. Whatever the reason, many of the books share a set of spiritual values which emphasize loving and helping other people. In *Green Light* by Lloyd Douglas religion gives a framework in which Episcopalian Dean Harcourt's ideas on how to live are set. He believes that God has ordained a "Long Parade" of life in which all people have a role to play. He feels that the whole of civilization is more important than any individual and that people should live their lives in terms of this whole, not just their daily traumas. And the contribution that all people can make to the "Long Parade" is love. Douglas puts forth a similar position in *Magnificent Obsession*. Here the characters work out a way of realizing and expanding the human personality: giving to others, with love. This is not far from the sort of ethic expressed by A. J. Cronin when he judges Dr. Manson good when he is helping poor patients and bad when he is trying to get into London society via rich patients.

Other books have remained closer to the twenties in their religious or spiritual views. Ty Ty Walden in *God's Little Acre* has made a personified God very human and love very physical:

> . . . when you get God in your heart, you have a feeling that living is worth striving for night and day: I ain't talking about the God you hear about in churches. I'm talking about the God inside of a body. I've got the greatest feeling for Him, because He helps me to live. That's why I set aside God's little acre out there on the farm. . . . That's the sign that God's in my heart.
>
> . . . You know good and well how tired I am when Sunday comes, after digging all week long in the holes. God don't miss me, anyhow. He knows why I can't come. I've spoken to Him about such things all my life, and He knows pretty well all about it.[23]

Not only does Ty Ty take God out of the church but he also thinks that God could teach about making love. When Buck is having trouble with his wife Griselda, Ty Ty recommends that he pray to his God:

> He can tell you things nobody else can, and maybe he'll tell you how you ought to act with Griselda. He'll tell you, if you'll only take the time and trouble to listen, because if there's anything in the world He's crazy about, it's seeing a man and a woman fools about each other. He knows then that the world is running along as slick as grease.[24]

Even his God is made earthy.

The two trends that express the strongest impulses expressed during this period are not irreconcilable. The spiritual love and the physical love are both presented as ways of making the life of ordinary people good in an ordinary, unexotic world. Perhaps a contrast made in *Lost Horizon* expresses this feeling as well as anything else does. Near the beginning of the book, Hilton describes the feelings of the leading character, Conway, who expresses the view held by many fictional characters in the middle thirties:

> The will of God or the lunacy of man—it seemed to him that you could make your choice, if you wanted a good enough reason for most things. Or, alternately . . . the will of man and the lunacy of God.[25]

Then Conway spends his time with the monks of Shangri-La, hidden in the Himalayas far away from the civilization he has known. The monks run their village on a principle of moderation in all things, allowing personal pleasure but not excesses that will hurt others. The life there is peaceful and, to Conway, beautiful. He comes to admire the monks and what they have done. Finally the head of the colony, Perrault, tells Conway that Shangri-La is to be a hidden place that will survive when the rest of the world is destroyed in war. He says further:

> Then, my son, when the strong have devoured each other, the Christian ethic may at last be fulfilled, and the meek shall inherit the earth.[26]

Despite the telling of the story in terms of a hide-away from the world's evils, Hilton evinces some faith that men can make the world a good place. His Western characters, by the end, are more good than bad.

Father Perrault's hope that the meek shall inherit the earth expresses the feeling conveyed in many of the books written between 1928 and 1937. Despite the New Deal, the novels do not express an interest in experimentation. A Hardingesque desire for normalcy is much more prevalent. Except for *God's Little Acre,* there is a little concern for the world outside the intimate world of the readers. They largely ignore the problems of poverty at home and rising totalitarianism abroad. Apparently they find these problems too large to tackle. Instead, this group of authors is proposing an answer to the question of the early and middle twenties. They try to provide an end to the search for meaning by asserting the primacy of being close to, loving, and helping other people. But in doing this, both authors and readers ignore the two most pressing problems of their age. All the questioning during the twenties failed to result in this group of people's committing themselves to anything outside themselves. The questions posed may have been too great for this group to continue asking long enough to find an answer. The problems of the rest of the world turned them inward on themselves. Tired of both responsibilities and questions, they needed reassurance and rest.

CHAPTER 5

THE WHODUNITS: ESCAPE AND REALISM

Best Selling Novels: 1926-1941

1926	Earl Derr Biggers, *The Chinese Parrot*
1926	Agatha Christie, *The Murder of Roger Ackroyd*
1927	Frances Noyes Hart, *The Bellamy Trial*
1927	S. S. Van Dine, *The Canary Murder Case*
1928	Earl Derr Diggers, *Behind That Curtain*
1929	Dashiell Hammett, *Red Harvest*
1929	S. S. Van Dine, *The Bishop Murder Case*
1930	E. C. Bentley, *Trent's Last Case*
1930	Earl Derr Biggers, *Charlie Chan Carries On*
1930	Dashiell Hammett, *The Maltese Falcon*
1930	Ellery Queen, *The French Powder Mystery*
1931	Leslie Charteris, *Enter the Saint*
1931	Dashiell Hammett, *The Glass Key*
1931	Ellery Queen, *The Dutch Shoe Mystery*
1932	Agatha Christie, *Peril at End House*
1932	Ellery Queen, *The Egyptian Cross Mystery*
1933	Erle Stanley Gardner, *The Case of the Sulky Girl*
1933	Erle S. Gardner, *The Case of the Velvet Claws*
1933	Erle S. Gardner, *The Case of the Lucky Legs*
1934	Erle S. Gardner, *The Case of the Curious Bride*
1934	Ellery Queen, *The Adventures of Ellery Queen*
1934	Ellery Queen, *The Chinese Orange Mystery*
1935	Erle S. Gardner, *The Case of the Caretaker's Cat*

1935 Erle S. Gardner, *The Case of the Counterfeit Eye*
1935 Ellery Queen, *The Spanish Cape Mystery*
1936 Erle S. Gardner, *The Case of the Stuttering Bishop*
1936 Jonathon Latimer, *Lady in the Morgue*
1936 Rex Stout, *The Rubber Band*
1937 Erle S. Gardner, *The Case of the Dangerous Dowager*
1937 Erle S. Gardner, *The Case of the Lame Canary*
1938 Erle S. Gardner, *The Case of the Substitute Face*
1938 Marco Page, *Fast Company*
1939 Eric Ambler, *A Coffin for Dimitrios*
1939 Leslie Charteris, *The Happy Highwayman*
1939 Agatha Christie, *Easy to Kill*
1940 Eric Ambler, *Journey Into Fear*
1940 Raymond Chandler, *Farewell, My Lovely*
1940 Agatha Christie, *And Then There Were None*
1940 Ellery Queen, *New Adventures of Ellery Queen*
1941 Agatha Christie, *The Patriotic Murders*

"Whodunit" is a popular misnomer for mystery stories. At the real base of the best selling mysteries lies an interest not so much in who committed the crime but in who solved it, what methods he used, and how invincible that hero is. The heroes of these mysteries are like the self-reliant men of the Depression novels. However, unlike the non-mystery novels, the plots of these stories center around the strong helping the weak. Many of them have a theme of social responsibility to the extent that the heroes see that justice is done to the individuals involved, both to the guilty and to the innocent who have been accused. The hero is the ever-present crusader who protects the weak who cannot look out for themselves, and he is self-fortified strength.

The majority of the mysteries resemble the Depression books in placing lower value on money than on love. Love rarely is so impure as to be the motive for murder. Instead, that motive is usually either desire for gain or the need to cover up a crime already committed. This contrast between money and emotion however is not presented in the sentimental manner that it was by such writers as Lloyd Douglas.

Despite their seemingly unintellectual qualities or perhaps because of them, the mysteries provide a link between the twenties, the thirties, and the forties. They reflect the exoticism of the twenties, the escapism of the thirties, and to a certain extent the realistic recognition of some of the complexity of the world that appears at the end of the thirties and in the forties.

In one technical aspect this group of mysteries differs from the other best sellers. Whereas most of the novels received their highest sale within the first few years after their publication, the mysteries did not. These mysteries appeared from 1926 to 1941, the majority of them during the thirties, but their heaviest sale occurred in the years immediately following 1939 when Pocket Books, Inc. went into business. In this way also, then, as well as in the area of values expressed, they form a link between the three decades.

The type of book was very popular. There are forty titles included in this category. Many of the authors of mysteries and their hero characters are repeaters. The fact of the continuing reappearance of the hero supports the contention that *he*, not the villain, is most important. The forty titles represent works by only thirteen authors. Three of these have five, seven, and ten titles apiece. The readers thus knew what to expect of their heroes.

The mysteries fall into two major categories: those in which the hero solves the crime mainly by the use of logic with only a minimum of violence and those in which the descriptions of violence play a major role in the narrative. The violent group are far fewer in number. These books were written at the beginning and at the end of the Depression. None were written in those harshest days of the mid-thirties. As was noted before, this fact does not reflect the period during which they sold the best. Whereas the deep Depression books had father-image heroes, the heroes of the books of violence seem rather to personify the little guy who has the right to do almost anything to protect himself. The heroes are not particularly intelligent. Above all, they are violent. Also, they do not stand above the other characters because of their own superior morality. In the violent mysteries, in fact, the largest difference between the heroes and the villains is the point of view from which the story is told. Most of the violent heroes are just as much out for their own material gain as are the villains.

There are eight books that fall strictly within this group. The Early Depression ones are three by Dashiell Hammett: *Red Harvest* (1929), *The Maltese Falcon* (1930), and *The Glass Key* (1931). The ones written at the end of the Depression are: *The Lady in the Morgue* (1937) by Jonathon Latimer, *Fast Company* (1938) by Marco Page, *Farewell, My Lovely* (1940) by Raymond Chandler, and *A Coffin for Dimitrios* (1939) and *Journey Into Fear* (1940) by Eric Ambler.

Rex Stout's *The Rubber Band* (1936) has a fair amount of violence, but its greater stress on qualities of the intellect precludes its being counted among the books in which violence rules and physical strength is the most necessary prerequisite for survival. Nero Wolfe, the detective, is devoted to orchids, beer, and logic. His obesity results in his hating all things physical. It is too unpleasant for him to move around. It is his assistant, Archie, who contributes the violence. Despite their tough talk, both have a tendency to undertake missions to help innocent, naive clients.

This description indicates the most general characteristic of the other group of mysteries. The heroes help the weak and the innocent when they are faced with an evil that is stronger than they are. Intelligence and reason predominate as the methods of solving crimes. These heroes thus have the same attributes as those of the thirties. However, they use their skills to assist others instead of concentrating on their own aggrandizement.

Leslie Charteris' books about the Saint, *Enter the Saint* (1930) and *The Happy Highwayman* (1939), resemble the other group of books in that no absolute distinctions are made between hero, victim, and villain. In fact, there are good crooks whom the Saint helps. These are basically nice people who happen to steal sometimes. This is the crook become victim. The Saint himself could, in fact, be considered a good law breaker in that he sometimes steals from the rich to give to the poor. He does not dress in green, but otherwise the image fits.

Charlie Chan stands as the opposite to the Saint. He is as straight as they come. Charlie, a proper middle class Honolulu Police Department detective sergeant, of Chinese origin and very traditionalist values, is the hero of the three books in the list by Earl Derr Biggers. These are: *The Chinese Parrot* (1926), *Behind That Curtain* (1928), and *Charlie Chan Carries On* (1930). Charlie aspires to neither money, nor fame, nor the hustle-bustle of the North American mainland. In many ways he resembles the more spiritually oriented characters of the thirties. Yet he is more realistic in his ability to recognize and deal with evil in the world.

S. S. Van Dine's novels, where the rich mingle with actresses and quack neurologists, reflect the exoticism of the twenties. His hero, Philo Vance, who gives the cynical line about being interested in the mystery as a game rather than for the good of the people involved, nevertheless always comes out on the side of right and justice. Van Dine is represented by two books: *The Canary Murder Case* (1927) and *The Bishop Murder Case* (1929).

Two books in this group are singles. Frances Noyes Hart's *The Bellamy Trial* (1927) shows the tragedy brought to many lives as the facts are brought out in a murder case. The harm done to innocent people in the revelation of their private lives is stressed above the sensationalism of the trial. *Trent's Last Case* (1930) by E. C. Bentley is the other single book by an author in the non-violent group. It is the last case of the detective because his logic does not lead to the solution of the murder on the large English estate. He finds out the true solution, quits his profession, and marries one of the female principals. In the end, justice is done. Trent learns that the murder was committed in self-defense, and so he keeps the secret.

Three authors remain. These three combined are responsible for over half of the best selling mysteries. They wrote twenty-two of the total forty. Of the twenty-two, Agatha Christie wrote five, Ellery Queen wrote seven, and Erle Stanley Gardner wrote ten. Although these authors and the characters they created vary considerably, they all share several qualities. As in the rest of the latter group of books, the heroes use their heads more than their hands. Furthermore, there is always some slight intellectual intrusion on the plot varying from Christie's Hercule Poirot's sociological interpretations of the English to Gardner's Perry Mason's knowledge of the fine points of the law. These heroes are incorruptible and all acknowledge some kind of abstract difference between good and evil. They are not, however, as absolutist as were some of the characters of the thirties. In all the mysteries, the acceptance of a variety of rather spicy characters resembles the attitude of the twenties when variety was also found interesting.

Agatha Christie wrote two types of books: those which star the Belgian detective Hercule Poirot and those which do not. Hercule is quaint, elderly, a snob of sorts, and yet kindly to innocents in trouble. He appears in *The Murder of Roger Ackroyd* (1926) where he lets the murderer commit suicide in order to escape the disgrace of trial and conviction. In *Peril at End House* (1932) Hercule saves a young girl from being falsely convicted of murder and allows the real killer to poison herself with opium. In *The Patriotic Murders* (1941) Poirot refuses to let an important international financier get away with murder. Poirot's derogatory remarks on much that is modern are humorous enough to leave the reader his choice about what he thinks of the modern world. Much of Poirot's verbal intolerance is not however backed up by his deeds.

There are two mysteries without Poirot. *Easy to Kill* (1939) is a Poirot type story set in an English town, starring the village aristocracy, many of them elderly. *And Then There Were None* (1940) is considerably more unique. Retired Justice Wargrave sentences nine untried murderers to die on an island he has acquired for that specific purpose. His murderers did things like letting a child drown and abandoning a group of natives to die while the English took off to safer ground, and abandoning a maid who is pregnant leaving her with no resources and therefore desperate enough to kill herself. This stresses a theme that runs throughout the detective stories: that is that the official law is not sufficient and that private just men must see to other people's well being.

The Ellery Queen books are another case of this approach. Police Inspector Queen is honest and respectable, but his free-lance, play-boyish son is brilliant and solves all the crimes and then writes about the adventure. Ellery Queen is the pen name for the two men who make up the stories. Queen is not only smart, but he has the advantage of being able to call out the whole New York Police Department to assist him when extra help is needed. The Queen stories tend to contain an element of the exotic exemplified by nudist colonies, rare statues from the Far East and plots turning on religious symbolism. Also there is usually a specific area of expertise with which Ellery must be somewhat familiar: medicine, archeology, or boating, for example. These are not experiences with which the average suburbanite could identify. Rather, they provide an escape into something slightly unknown. Nothing, however, appears unknown to the omniscient Ellery, and he succeeds in solving everybody's problems. Most of the Ellery Queen books included in this study were written during the most difficult period of the Depression and, like the other books, had their best sale when they first came out in the Pocket Book edition. They are: *The French Powder Mystery* (1930), *The Dutch Shoe Mystery* (1931), *The Egyptian Cross Mystery* (1932), *The Adventures of Ellery Queen* (1934), *The Chinese Orange Mystery* (1934), *The Spanish Cape Mystery* (1935), and *The New Adventures of Ellery Queen* (1940).

The best selling writer of all those who wrote best sellers from 1914 to 1945 was Erle Stanley Gardner. His Perry Mason books sold into the millions, several million per title,[1] and he produced them in great quantity. Ten are included in this study. They are: *The Case of the Sulky Girl* (1933), *The Case of the Velvet Claws* (1933), *The Case of the Curious Bride* (1934), *The Case of the Lucky Legs* (1934), *The Case of the Caretaker's Cat* (1935), *The Case of the Counterfeit Eye* (1935), *The Case of the Stuttering Bishop* (1936), *The Case of the Dangerous Dowager* (1937), *The Case of the Lame Canary* (1937), *The Case of the Substitute Face* (1938).

Like the Ellery Queen stories, the Perry Mason adventures were written during the depth of the Depression. Unlike the Ellery Queen stories, they do not usually provide particularly exotic characters and settings. Perry is a lawyer, and his clients are usually fairly normal people. They are people that most of the readers could recognize. There is a formula to these stories. Perry's client, usually likeable, always innocent, is unjustly accused of murder. Perry secures his client's release, during the course of a trial, by providing the evidence to convict the real killer. These stories, instead of providing escape, show what one man's intelligence and determination can do. Perry thus is like many characters in other Depression books, but he also represents very well the acceptance in the best sellers of the forties of the strong looking out for the weak. Perry explains to his detective assistant:

> A person is accused of crime, and immediately the whole law-enforcement machinery gets busy unearthing evidence to prove he's guilty. When he tries

to get evidence to prove he's innocent, he runs up against a brick wall.[2]

Perry always finds the way to circumvent that brick wall.

These then briefly are the mysteries and their heroes. Since they do provide such a combination of the twenties, thirties, and forties, they can be used as a source for picking out some constants that continued, at least in part, from the late twenties through World War II. Certainly the books of less violent, more rational, more helpful emphases are more typical than the others.

Some sociological explanations of the success of the mysteries have been put forward. Christopher La Farge has suggested that in the violent mysteries men see justice "meted out without delay."[3] The process is only slightly more prolonged in the less violent books. Charles J. Rolo describes the mystery stories as "compensatory daydreams" to relieve the frustration caused by the increasing awareness of mass evils, such as war, Nazism, and crime networks.[4] Hortense Powdermaker makes a similar interpretation of suspense movies. She asserts that they relieve general tension by creating a specific cause of anxiety and then solving it.[5] Alfred Kazin asserted that 1929 restored consciousness of reality, and he said further that there was a new social realism in an attempt to meet the crisis.[6] The mysteries certainly give acknowledgement to the fact that there is a seamy side of life.

Leo Gurko provides an explanation for the popularity of the tough guy, the hero of the more violent mysteries. He describes him as the modern day cowboy, the rugged individual. The tough guy or the gangster, Gurko asserts, is making an independent gesture of defiance against the established pattern in a world where all is still a competition for survival.[7] Gurko presents this in an amoral context. All this might suggest that there is a basic difference between the readers of the violent books, who see or want to see the world as Gurko suggests it is, and the readers of the books in which right rather than might wins. This latter group would also see the contest but would believe that the world is not amoral and that right does or should prevail in the end.

The mysteries almost by definition have more in common than the other groups of books because their plots are all based around one similar central theme. Aside from the basic difference in world outlook mentioned above, it would be logical for the mysteries to share other similarities that grow out of this basic structure. Many categories which show important developments in the best selling novels are significant here only because they are not considered. A comparison with the other groups of novels will show the differences and similarities in emphasis.

The authors of the mysteries ranged in age from 26 to 55, roughly the same average age group as the authors of the non-mystery best sellers of the thirties. They were born between 1875 and 1909, a slightly longer period than that during which the authors of the latter group were born. This is to be expected since the books were written over a longer time period. Of the thirteen authors, only two were born in the Northeast, but these are the most popular two, Gardner and Queen. Three were born in the South or border states. Three were born in the Middle West. Three were born in England and one in Singapore. For one, Marco Page, the information is not available. Like the writers of the novels of the thirties, this group represents a disproportionately large number of Southerners and foreigners. In the mysteries, however, a large amount of the action takes place in the Northeastern part of the United States.

The mysteries are comparatively short. They all run under 400 pages. This is unlike the trend toward long books that was strong during the thirties. All of the mysteries are contemporary and are highly realistic. Most of the books are set in New York City, California, or England. Except for the English small towns that Poirot haunts (none of them too far from London), and a few jaunts to American beaches, they are all highly urbanized.

The vocabulary and style of all the mysteries is fairly straightforward. Like the plots and settings, they are easily comprehended by the urban and suburban middle class reader. Although some of the detectives employ technical vocabularies, these expressions are always defined to include the reader in the area of expertise. A few of the detectives use foreign phrases which may or may not be defined. Only very slight use is made even of regional and class dialects, perhaps implying that a person's region of origin and class mattered less than whether or not he was a criminal or whose side he was on.

A large number of the mysteries have some moderate element of humor. Most of the humor comes in day-to-day interaction, the funny mannerisms of the characters. Some comes through attacks on accepted values or authorities, including the police, and some in making fun of individuals. There is little family humor or ethnic humor.

The most important generalization about style is that these are books of action. This is also different from the novels written at the same time. Many of those contain long, abstract discussions of morality, what is the good life, and other complex subjects. Any such abstractions presented in the mysteries usually are no more than two or three sentence remarks. The Perry Mason books probably contain more of these than most others. This one will illustrate their brevity. Perry comments on his return from Hawaii:

> It's been a wonderful interlude, but *I* want to start fighting. Over there . . . is something which civilization has commercialized but can't kill, a friendly people, a gentle warm climate, where time drifts by unnoticed. I'm leaving it to go back to the roar of a city, the jangle of telephones, the blast of automobile horns, the clanging of traffic signals, clients who lie to me and yet expect me to be loyal to them—and I can hardly wait to get there.[8]

This is one of the most completely spelled out explanations of motives in any of the mysteries. This passage also illustrates the urban commitment in most of them.

The mysteries then are generally compact and emphasize action, yet they contain a high degree of respect for individuals, for individual achievement. They also evidence considerable feeling of responsibility of the strong for the weak and for the strong to uphold a certain order in society.

As in other best sellers, international and national politics play almost no role in the mysteries,[9] entering into almost none of them. Local politics and local government, however, do play a role. In fact, there is more interest in local politics and government in the mysteries than there is in any other group of books. This is another way in which the stories are closer to the experiences of ordinary readers. Almost everybody has some contact with the police and often with other representatives of the local government.

Since these make up such a large part of the references to local politics, the points of view expressed here are of particular interest. In a few books, especially the Ellery Queen books, the most prominent representative of local political forces, the police department, is presented favorably. The police there are generally honest, hard-working, and willing to cooperate with Ellery whom they usually have the sense to acknowledge is more intelligent than they are.

Far more frequently, in nineteen of the books, local government is characterized all the way from being not too intelligently run, in need of reform, to corrupt. In the Perry Mason books, Perry usually winds up the book with a courtroom duel with District Attorney Hamilton Burger. Burger and the police are honest, but they always try to convict on evidence that is not complete. In this case, stupidity would lead to a miscarriage of justice if Perry were not there to thwart the less intelligent civil servants. Nero Wolfe, Rex Stout's detective, is contemptuous of the police because of their stupidity. His assistant Archie describes one police captain as "one of the lower animals."[10] S. S. Van Dine's detective Philo Vance blames governmental inefficiency on its popular control. When the District Attorney complains that the newspapers are hounding him to produce a murderer before he has had the time to find the right man, Vance reminds him:

> You forget, my dear chap, . . . that we are living under the benign and upliftin' reign of Democritus, which confers upon every ignoramus the privilege of promiscuously criticizing his betters.[11]

Most books criticize individual stupidity rather than making an outright attack on our total system of government. Leslie Charteris comments in *The Happy Highwayman*: "The Law, in the Saint's opinion, was a stodgy and elephantine institution. . . ."[12] He feels this was because he knows so many stodgy enforcers of the law. E. C. Bentley's detective Trent had a similar opinion:

> . . . the cleverest criminals seldom run to strategic subtlety. When they do, they don't get caught, since clever policemen have if possible less strategic subtlety than the ordinary clever criminal.[13]

Generally the heroes think the police are rather stupid, and in the stories they are portrayed as such.

Several books illustrate different kinds of miscarriage of justice. *And Then There Were None* shows that the law is not sufficient to punish all guilty people by describing the guilt of many whom the law could not reach. *The Bellamy Trial*, on the other hand, tells of the personal cruelty to people connected with a trial in which two innocent people were accused. Many damaging personal affairs had to be exposed to prove the innocence of the accused. It must be noted though that this is one of the few books which shows that the law is not always rigid. The real murderer, an elderly woman who is going to die in a year, writes a letter of confession to the judge who burns it rather than prosecuting her.

Local government is presented at its worst when it is corrupt. Leslie Charteris presents this in a humorous fashion when the Saint forces a crooked politician who is making a fortune on graft to give a lot of money to charity. Dashiell Hammett and Jonathon Latimer include drunken detectives, incompetent officials, and gangs as an integral part of the city political scene. Hammett's *The Glass Key* is about the fight for the political control of a city. The two opposing groups are almost equally corrupt although "the bad guys" are slightly more gangsterish in their techniques. A murder is used as a political tool, one side trying to blame it on the other in order to discredit them at the polls. The characters are ruthless both physically and emotionally. The politicians have no higher ideals. Their only goals are power and wealth.

The mysteries then focus on the local, the familiar, in politics and political people. And the judgment of the local governmental scene varies from finding the people well intentioned but mildly incompetent as in Ellery Queen to portraying them as absolute villains as Dashiell Hammett does. One way in which the mystery stories are more realistic than many of the non-mystery stories is in their characterization of local politics and government. The characters both good and bad recognize that both must be dealt with rather than shunned. That is a step toward realism, toward coming to grips with the world.

On questions of race, the mystery stories are less realistic. Racial matters are, in fact, largely ignored. The leading characters are almost always Anglo-Saxon and nominal Protestants (except for several European Catholics), always whites except for Charlie Chan. They pay little heed to the existence of minorities and, where they do notice them, it is usually in the most stereotyped way.

The few Negroes who appear at all are always in the position of a servant or menial worker. Those few generally speak a dialect. For example, in Ellery Queen's *The French Powder Mystery*, a black woman, whom the whites call a coon, went to clean a store window's exhibition bedroom one morning and found a body dead in the bed. When asked if she expected to find the body, she replied: "Nossuh! Ah wouldn't 'a' teched dat bed fo' a thousan' dollahs if Ah'd know dat!"[14] Ellery Queen in another book, however, does make a point of teaching his servant Djuna to say Negro instead of nigger.

The position in society held by Negroes is expressed quite well by a policeman in *Fast Company.* A lawyer has come into the police department and is jesting with the officer on duty. The lawyer says: "I came for some justice. . . ." The police officer then asks: "You want our special white well-to-do justice, or just the kind we hand out to niggers and strikers?"[15]

Agatha Christie in *And Then There Were None* presents the position most favorable to black people. One of the judge's unpunished murderers was a Mr. Lombard who was leading a party in Africa. When he was threatened, he abandoned twenty Africans to their death. He considered them just natives; the judge considered them men. This book appeared in 1940 when readers apparently were beginning to be more aware of social problems. Other than these few examples, there is no consideration given to Negroes.

Jews get far less treatment than Negroes, but it is hardly more favorable. In *Fast Company*, the most villainous characters are Abe Seligman and Elizabeth Bannerman, both obviously Jewish. They are greedy. One Perry Mason book, *The Case of the Caretaker's Cat*, has a crooked lawyer with a Jewish name, Nat Shuster, but no reference is made to his being Jewish, and other Gardner characters have other Jewish names without being particularly corrupt.

Southern and Eastern Europeans fare roughly the same way as Jews. Ellery Queen in *The Egyptian Cross Mystery* generalizes about the Balkans, calling them the "heart of superstition and violence."[16] S. S. Van Dine in *The Bishop Murder Case* describes racial facial types: "His mouth, too, was firm and clean-cut, but it held a look of cynical cruelty which was more Mediterranean than Nordic."[17] Characters in *Red Harvest* talk about Dagos. Characters in *The Lady in the Morgue* call Italians Wops and Filipinos greaseballs. Because of their international settings and characters, Eric Ambler's stories would seem a likely place for similar stereotyping, but there is none. His mixture of nationalities results only in good and bad individuals. It is perhaps noteworthy that *A Coffin for Dimitrios* was written in 1939 and *Journey Into Fear* in 1940.

The one case in which a different racial-nationality group is presented favorably is in the Charlie Chan stories. Charlie supports the traditional Chinese way of living as opposed to the hustle and bustle of modern America. He makes comments such as this one:

> Chinese knows he is one minute grain of sand on seashore of eternity. With what result? He is calm and quiet and humble. No nerves, like hopping, skipping Caucasian. Life for him not so much ordeal.[18]

Despite his broken English, Charlie is always acknowledged to be the most intelligent man around. Also, the author allows it to sneak out that Charlie really is not so different, that he is fairly well Americanized. His daughter is in college in California. Charlie himself admits in *Charlie Chan Carries On* that his restlessness between important cases is probably due to the fact that he is becoming Americanized.

Despite this one great Chinese character, the mysteries show almost no social concern in any area connected with race. As reflected in the mysteries, racism in America was not destroyed in the thirties as Oscar Handlin suggested it was.[19] This may also reflect the wider reading audience afforded the mysteries by their large paperback sale. Probably it is the case that many readers of the other best sellers read mysteries, but many other people read mysteries to whom social reforming would not be of interest.

The characters in the mysteries are not only largely white and Protestant but also of middle class background. There are a few members of the upper class. Little specific discussion is made of class relationships. Certainly, in comparison to the plot, they are of little importance. It is significant that lower class characters almost never have important roles. They are largely ignored except where they have been witnesses to a crime. They are not fully drawn characters. The few upper class characters appear most frequently in the stories of S. S. Van Dine, Leslie Charteris, Ellery Queen, and Agatha Christie. Their detectives are all socially upper class people. In these books, the detectives are rather aristocratic: they are all men of leisure who solve crimes because of the fun of the puzzle. S. S. Van Dine's Philo Vance once says: "Really, y'know, I'm no avenger of society, but I do detest an unsolved problem."[20] He and the others like him are conscious of their education and social position and sometimes consider the masses a bit vulgar, but this never affects their professional objectivity. In fact, these men are so aristocratic that money has little appeal. Rich people appear in most of the other books, but without the trappings of aristocratic culture. The possession of money makes little difference in the character of the people. Rich characters can be good or bad. The only real value judgment made is that people should not kill in order to get money. The people that do this killing to gain incidentally are never faced with starvation. They are portrayed as merely greedy.

Perry Mason is a slightly different case. He has a lot of money, most of it earned, but not the upper class cultural interests. He charges high fees to clients who can afford it, particularly if they are nasty, but he works just as hard for clients he knows cannot pay. Perry and Della, his secretary, believe in hard work. This attitude is slightly different from the puzzle-playing of the more aristocratic detectives. Also, they are more interested in justice as an abstract goal, not justice as a secondary result of solving a puzzle. Charlie Chan resembles Perry Mason in this way. These are the professionals.

Neither the upper class amateur detectives nor the middle class professionals are interested primarily in personal gain. The only detectives that have this interest are those in the novels of violence. Where the detectives spend a lot of time in the severe physical fighting with the guilty, they tend also to be involved in the same acquisitive battle. The characters of Hammett, Latimer, Page, and Chandler are all out after money. This extreme pursuit of money is condemned in the non-violent books. It must be noted, however, that in all books, except the violent ones, the heroes are well established financially. Since the majority of the mystery heroes fall into the categories of amateur or middle class non-violent, both monied, it would appear that most of the readers prefer to identify with those who have money rather than those who do not.

In the consideration of the role of class in the mysteries, it must be noted that if the lower class makes little contribution to the solution of crimes, neither are they held responsible for crimes. They are simply missing. The guilty characters can be anything from secretaries to industrialists, missionaries to professional confidence men and dope sellers. The untrained, unskilled poor are just left out. Their crimes apparently are not considered interesting enough to be the material of a novel.

Despite certain differences in the characters of the detectives, in all the mysteries innate skill possessed by the hero is more important than hard work. Most of the detectives are presented as knowing that some hard work is necessary to solve the crime, but, in all the books, no amount of diligence could possibly make up for a lack of native intelligence. This indicates a belief in a natural elite. Education is generally considered good, but not of overriding importance. The upper class amateurs and middle class professional detectives are all well educated, but it is shown to be their skill, not their training, which makes them always victorious. All of this expresses the philosophy that those best equipped intellectually do prevail over their inferiors. This is an aristocracy not of the rich but of the talented.

The roles of art and nature have been discussed in all the other chapters at this point. It must be noted that there is no place for such a discussion here since the mysteries are too strongly oriented towards action for these to have any place.

The emphasis on action in these books may be seen as a beginning reassertion of vitality after the Depression. Furthermore, the characters in the mysteries, in their ability to deal with crime and in their recognition of the conditions of local politics, indicate a turning back to acceptance of reality. It appears that the refusal to do this in the novels of the period 1928 to 1937 has run its course. The acceptance of reality has been accompanied by a growing social conscience, a factor that was lacking in the novels of the Depression years. Although the mysteries generally ignored racial problems, the presence of Charlie Chan as a hero provides an indication of change that would follow in the 1940s. This is also true of the fact that in the mysteries the strong feel a responsibility to care for the weak. Because many of the mysteries with these characteristics were written during the thirties, they provide a valuable link between the novels of the Depression and those that followed in the forties.

The mysteries do not place the importance on family relations that many of the non-mystery novels do. Only two of the major heroes have any kind of family relations at all. These are Charlie Chan, who is very concerned with his family, and Ellery Queen who works closely with and respects his father. Perry Mason, Hercule Poirot, the Saint, and many of the lesser detectives are "loners."

Although the two detectives with families live harmoniously with them, the largest reflection of family life comes from the transitory characters involved in the novels, and they rarely have a tranquil family life. Relations between children and parents are portrayed more frequently than any other sort of family dealings. Perhaps this is because of the intimate connection this relationship has with the passing on of the family money. Parents and their children have their most difficult times in the violent books. Many of the characters in these stories have no interest in family at all. In one, *The Glass Key*, Senator Henry kills his son, Taylor. No other conflict has that extreme result. In the less violent books there are also strong conflicts between parents and children. In one Ellery Queen book a stepson plots to kill his stepfather. In another, a mother has an affair with the man her daughter is in love with. In Erle Stanley Gardner's books, often family members desire to hurt each other for reasons of passion, but usually someone else commits the murder for reasons of greed. There is a particularly unhealthy relationship in S. S. Van Dine's *The Bishop Murder Case.* A Professor Dillard is jealous of younger Professor Arnesson's affections for his daughter. He commits a series of murders for which he hopes Arnesson will be blamed. In other books, there are other examples of families whose members exhibit the total range of behavior towards each other, but in most of them the idea is put forward that family harmony is preferable and leads to greater happiness.

This same thing is true of marital relations. Most of the

authors present examples of both good and bad marriages. The characters enjoying good marriages are generally strong and happy people. Those suffering from bad marriages are sad and sometimes evil, but not necessarily so. Divorce has been accepted. Many of the characters have been or are getting a divorce. Also, extra-marital affairs are accepted. Eighteen of the books contain examples of such affairs. Generally no judgment is made of these in terms of absolute right or wrong. They are accepted as a fact of existence. Perry Mason, who is comparatively conservative in his social ethics, makes a pronouncement of the subject of divorce:

> Hundreds of thousands of marriages go on the rocks every year, but that doesn't mean that either or both parties to the divorce action are not ordinary likeable human beings. It simply means that emotions don't remain static; that love, like any other fire, will burn itself out unless fresh fuel is added.[21]

This speaks for the attitude towards divorce and also adultery in most of the novels. Some people even expect marriage to fail. Ellery Queen at one point tells two of his friends who are getting married:

> I trust you'll both be very happy, but I doubt it. . . . Oh, . . . don't take that personally. I was making the usual misogynist's observation about marriage.[22]

All of these negative statements reflect both a growing realism about marriage as a personal relation and the acceptance of changing social patterns, including the unwillingness to judge people who do not conform to any specific standard. Not only the bad marriage, but the neutral one is also described. This is written about Graham in Eric Ambler's *Journey Into Fear:*

> It had never occurred to him to doubt that his attitude towards his wife was that of any other man towards a wife to whom he had been married for ten years. He had married her because he was tired of living in furnished rooms, and had assumed (correctly) that she had married him to get away from her father.[23]

All of these negative feelings are accepted. What is not condoned is a criminal act. In Latimer's *The Lady in the Morgue* Udoni kills his wife. This is not accepted. In Christie's *The Murder of Roger Ackroyd* Mrs. Ferrars has poisoned her husband.

She metes out her own punishment by committing suicide. In Christie's *The Patriotic Murders* a rich industrialist named Blunt murders several people to hide the fact that he is a bigamist. Poirot turns him in.

Bad marriages lead to other bad things besides murder. In Perry Mason's *The Case of the Curious Bride*, Carl Montaine tries to frame his wife Rhoda and have her convicted for a murder which neither of them committed. In another Perry Mason book, *The Case of the Sulky Girl*, Mrs. Mayfield, a housekeeper, gives her justification for blackmail:

> All my life I've been a working woman. I've married a husband who is a clod, and hasn't the ambition or sense enough to come in out of the rain.[24]

This reasoning is not accepted.

In summary, then, family relations are considered to bring happiness when they are good, but there is no condemnation of unhappy marriages, divorce, or extramarital affairs. None of these, however, are excusable grounds for breaking the law.

Despite the existence in these stories of many affairs, pre-marital as well as extra-marital, the description of them emphasizes the emotional, not the physical aspects. There is almost no physical description of anything vaguely connected with sex. The following three examples are typical. In *Journey Into Fear*, Graham wants to kiss a woman named Josette who is not his wife. The urge is described, but the kiss is not. In *Red Harvest*, some women are openly called mistress and brothels are called by name. At the end of *The Case of the Velvet Claws*, Perry and Della Street, his secretary, kiss each other. This is very unusual for them despite the fact that Perry has proposed to Della. Most certainly the appeal of the mysteries has no pornographic content. This is one of the traditional characteristics of the mysteries which are such a mixture of the traditional and the new.

Another traditionalist point of view they reflect is the idea that men are predominant over women. In all the books, without exception, the central character who does the crime-solving is a man. Because of their central position, men also are usually dominant over women. It is not, however, an unreasonable or oppressive domination. The fact is merely that the men are more important. In almost all of the books, however, women work and play an active role in the world outside the home. Generally there are some distinctions drawn about the levels of emotional and physical strength between men and women, with men the stronger, of course.

Almost all of the characters in the mysteries fall into an age group between young adult and middle age. They are mature people but, in general, young enough to retain their physical strength. Poirot is the only one of the major detectives who is too old to get involved in physical conflicts at least occasionally. In the violent books, physical strength is quite important and often is a main source of the detective's power. In the non-violent books physical strength is not the primary factor, but the hero must be able to defend himself if necessary. Roughly one-fourth of the books make the point that old age means physical decay. The shunning of older characters implies also a shunning of physical weakness.

In sixteen of the books, there is some kind of difference between old and young which causes tension. Generally the serious disputes are over one of two things: money and love. Where there is a different philosophy of life and the older generation is trying to hold down the younger, the younger usually prevails. In the mysteries, the young people go out in the world where they are what they are and do what they want. Generally they do not meet too much opposition from their elders when they try to do this, therefore the tension between the generations here is not as great as it is in other groups of books.

In these books of action, the beliefs of the characters are not generally set forward in a direct way. Only rarely do the authors break into the action to announce the philosophy of some character. One thing is immediately clear, however, from the plots. All of the detectives are optimists or, put another way, have faith in their own capabilities. They occassionally bow to modesty and express their doubts, but the reader knows their abilities and is certain that they will win. Generally they believe that they will come out on the top, and they do. This is a belief in self and not a reflection of some abstract principle which motivates them.

One other immediate generalization can be made. Religion is never a major factor in motivating the characters' actions. In none of the books does religion have more than a minor role and more often than not it is not even a minor influence. None of the detectives go to church. They are not preaching rebellion or atheism. No one even expects them to be religious, so there is nothing to rebel against.

Just as formal religion is missing, so are any formalized expectations about what man or men should be. Most of the books consider that men can be good and bad. There is little generalizing about human nature being good or evil. There are no complete reversals in character. Those who are very evil are apprehended, not converted. Many minor characters are allowed to get away with lesser breakages of the law without punishment. There is little interest in why people are good or evil. The problem of free will versus determinism is usually not brought into these mysteries. The motivations behind criminal acts are usually not need of any sort, so the problem of sociological causes of crime rarely enters in. There are some exceptions, however, to this generalization which indicate that a few of the writers are slightly sympathetic with the criminal. In *Fast Company* Joel, who is acting as the detective, sympathizes with a secretary who has pulled some fast deals to make some money on the side. He comments: "It's hell to be poor."[25] Later, when he finds out that she is also a murderer, he does not approve.

There is an even more complete explanation for the behavior of a villain in *A Coffin for Dimitrios.* The detective Latimer first thinks of Dimitrios as Evil and then decides that no judgment can be made:

> But it was useless to try to explain him in terms of Good and Evil. They were no more than baroque abstractions. . . . Dimitrios was not Evil. He was logical and consistent; as logical and consistent in the European jungle as the poison gas called Lewisite and the shattered bodies of children killed in the bombardment of an open town.[26]

His behavior is caused by his environment.

Severe judgment is usually reserved for those who commit severe crimes. There certainly is none against private matters like love affairs. There is generally condemnation of activities which endanger other people: murder, blackmail, dope peddling, and sometimes robbery. Sometimes an explanation moderates the judgment. In several Poirot books there are circumstances under which he condones murder. Also, the Saint robs the corrupt rich to give to the poor. In *The Bellamy Trial*, Mrs. Ives after confessing is allowed to live out her life. Some crimes apparently are worse than others. Some actions are presented as justifiable when they are caused by emotions and are condemned when caused by greed.

One author goes so far as to describe the potential for crime as something that exists in all of us. Philo Vance in S. S. Van Dine's *The Canary Murder Case* says:

> Everyone's a murderer at heart. The person who has never felt a passionate hankering to kill some one is without emotions. And do you think it's ethics or theology that stays the average person from homicide? Dear no! It's lack of courage—the fear of being found out, or haunted, or cursed with remorse. . . . Nations declare war against one another on the slightest provocation, so they can, with impunity, vent their lust for slaughter.[27]

This sort of comment is rare.

In the end, then, several conclusions can be drawn about the mystery stories. They do connect the social ethics of the thirties and forties and reveal the ambivalence of both periods in their combining strong individualism with an ethic of protecting the weak. They bear the qualities of exoticism and escapism of the twenties and thirties but they generally have some redeeming social point to make for those readers who care to notice it. One important condition is that this choice is left largely to the reader.

Probably the most important change reflected in this group of mysteries is a meshing of the twenties and thirties. Unlike many of the novels of the twenties, the mysteries do contain a good that is to win out, but that good is a more tolerant, less formalized, more worldly good than appears in most of the novels of the thirties. The trend as reflected in these best sellers then is away from both experimentalism and simplicity toward a truer and more complex definition of the culture.

CHAPTER 6

MATURATION: ACCEPTANCE OF REALITY

Best Selling Novels: 1938-1945

1938	Max Brand, *Singing Guns*
1938	Daphne DuMaurier, *Rebecca*
1938	Rachel Field, *All This, and Heaven Too*
1938	Ruth McKenney, *My Sister Eileen*
1938	Marjorie Kennan Rawlings, *The Yearling*
1938	Damon Runyon, *The Best of Damon Runyon*
1939	Sholen Asch, *The Nazarene*
1939	Christopher Morley, *Kitty Foyle*
1939	John Steinbeck, *The Grapes of Wrath*
1939	Ethel Vance, *Escape*
1940	Ernest Hemingway, *For Whom the Bell Tolls*
1940	Eric Knight, *Lassie-Come-Home*
1940	Richard Llewellyn, *How Green Was My Valley*
1940	Kenneth Roberts, *Oliver Wiswell*
1940	Jan Struther, *Mrs. Miniver*
1941	A. J. Cronin, *The Keys of the Kingdom*
1941	James Hilton, *Random Harvest*
1941	Helen MacInnes, *Above Suspicion*
1941	Alice Duer Miller, *The White Cliffs of Dover*
1941	Mary O'Hara, *My Friend Flicka*
1941	Ben Ames Williams, *Strange Woman*
1942	Pearl Buck, *Dragon Seed*
1942	Marcia Davenport, *The Valley of Decision*

1942 Lloyd Douglas, *The Robe*
1942 Damon Runyon, *Damon Runyan Favorites*
1942 Marguerite Steen, *The Sun Is My Undoing*
1942 John Steinbeck, *The Moon Is Down*
1942 Franz Werfel, *The Song of Bernadette*
1943 Sholem Asch, *The Apostle*
1943 Rose Franken, *Claudia*
1943 John Marquand, *So Little Time*
1943 Rosamond Marshall, *Kitty*
1943 William Saroyan, *The Human Comedy*
1943 Betty Smith, *A Tree Grows in Brooklyn*
1944 A. J. Cronin, *The Green Years*
1944 Elizabeth Goudge, *Green Dolphin Street*
1944 Gwethalyn Graham, *Earth and High Heaven*
1944 John Hersey, *A Bell for Adano*
1944 Somerset Maugham, *The Razor's Edge*
1944 Anya Seton, *Dragonwyck*
1944 Margery Sharp, *Cluny Brown*
1944 Lillian Smith, *Strange Fruit*
1944 Ben Ames Williams, *Leave Her to Heaven*
1945 Thomas B. Costain, *The Black Rose*
1945 James Hilton, *So Well Remembered*
1945 Adria Locke Langley, *A Lion Is In the Streets*
1945 Sinclair Lewis, *Cass Timberlane*
1945 Samuel Shellabarger, *Captain From Castile*
1945 James Ramsey Ullman, *The White Tower*
1945 Kathleen Winsor, *Forever Amber*

World War II marks the maturing of America as reflected in the values expressed in the best selling novels. The novels of the war years and those just preceding it reveal a final recognition of and acceptance of the complexity of reality. No longer do the books make only one point. They are complicated. Often political, religious, economic and personal problems are all intertwined in the same story. No longer are these different elements isolated or shown as unconnected. Now, the novels point out, social issues explicitly affect the individual. The quality, content and style of popular writing have become much closer to those of serious literary works than they have been during any previous time period.

It is difficult to generalize about the best sellers of the period beyond a statement of their complexity. The number of books that deal with problems of the lower income group reveals a time lag in the development of social conscience, for one would have expected to find these published during the Depression. There is a strong recognition that political matters can severely affect people's lives. For the first time a large number of novels deal with political questions. This is not solely a reaction to our participation in World War II as the tendency begins in 1938. Hitler's rapid expansion was making war in Europe almost inevitable, but we were not necessarily committed to participation. Also, the books express concern with both domestic and international politics. The best sellers of this period reveal an obvious concern with religion, the values and support it can yield, yet there is also much criticism of the hypocrisy in formal religion.

Many of the old battles have clearly been won. Freedom of language, sexual activities, and religious belief is accepted throughout. There is some discussion of personal preferences, but there is little attempt to impose these as absolute morality. The new propagandizing is against prejudice and in favor of political involvement.

An America which had faced the Depression and, during most of this period, had to deal with the twin horrors of Nazism and a world war, could no longer be comforted by books of escape or by the simplistic reassertion of tradition so prevalent in the novels of the earlier thirties. The realities of the world's complexity had been driven home in a most powerful fashion. The best sellers of this period 1938 to 1945 reveal a final, if belated, acceptance of these complexities and, of more importance, a willingness to come to grips with the problems.

There were fifty titles written between 1938 and 1945 which were best sellers. Many of these appeared quickly in Pocket Book editions. This indicates both that people were reading more and that more people were reading. For the most part, Pocket Books chose already popular books to reprint in its low cost editions, so it cannot be asserted that these best sellers represent a change from the fact that the best sellers were determined by the middle, upper middle, and upper classes. What can be asserted is that the new readers apparently accepted those values which the older group of readers now found appealing.

The most easily identifiable group of books produced during this period are those in which the plots center around World War II. Notably these all are concerned with the war in Europe. The first of these, *Escape*, appeared in 1939. Its plot centered on rescuing a woman from her Nazi imprisoners. *Mrs. Miniver* is about the brave approach to the war by an English family and shows how profoundly all English people were touched by the war. *Above Suspicion* is a spy story. The villains are Nazis. English bravery and wits prevail over Nazi strength. *The White Cliffs of Dover* recounts the acceptance by an American woman whose English husband had been killed in World War I of sending her son to fight for England in World War II. She realizes the importance of the cause. *The Moon Is Down* shows the bravery of the people of a small Norwegian town as they continue to resist the Nazis despite brutal retaliation. *A Bell for Adano* is the story of Major Joppolo as he commands the American military government in an occupied Italian town. It shows the good that can be done by well-intentioned American officers and the harm that can be done by the others. The last of the books of which the plot centers around the war is *The White Tower.* In this book, the leading characters leave the safety of Switzerland to rejoin the war effort, hoping that they will meet later in a better world. The plot lines of these books follow the course of the war. The early books are propaganda efforts in favor of American entry, then in support of the war effort. The later ones are concerned with what the world will be like after the war is over. It should be stated that many of the other books involve the war, but these are not included here because other elements in them are of equal or more importance.

A smaller major group of the novels of this period centers around religion. As soldiers began to be killed, some readers perhaps hoped to find comfort in belief in religious ideas, especially in the existence of an afterlife. Three of the four religiously centered books appeared in 1942 and 1943, the middle of the war. *The Nazarene* appeared earlier, in 1939. This is a sort of reinterpretation of the life of Christ seen partially through Jewish eyes. *The Robe* recounts the conversions to Christianity made by the robe taken from Christ when He was crucified. *The Song of Bernadette* is the life of the saint, particularly the struggle to gain recognition of her sainthood. *The Apostle* is a version of the life of St. Paul. All four of these works are long and very detailed. It is impossible to determine with any certainty whether their popularity was a result of the trauma of war or whether it represents a continuation to the return to spirituality that took place during the thirties. These books do, however, represent a distinct minority of the total group. The question will be discussed further later in the chapter.

The largest single group of books is that in which the ideals of social reform play a major role. The central themes are: the hardship of the economically underprivileged and some attempts at reform, the recognition of the difficulties of members of racial and religious minority groups, and the problem of rejection or acceptance of lower class or minority group characters by the rest. Many of the books in this group contain elements of both ethnic and economic concern. Thus they cannot be divided into two separate groups. Since the values involved will be analyzed at length, only the titles are listed here. This group then includes: *Singing Guns, Kitty Foyle, The Grapes of Wrath, How Green Was My Valley, For Whom the Bell Tolls, The Keys of the Kingdom, The Sun Is My Undoing, The Valley of Decision, Kitty, A Tree Grows in Brooklyn, The Green Years, Earth and High Heaven, Cluny Brown, Strange Fruit, The Black Rose, A Lion Is In the Streets,* and *Captain From Castile.* In all of these books, the conflict resulting from religious, ethnic or economic differences plays a major part in the plot.

Another group of books can be characterized merely as presenting a world which is complex in many ways, economic, racial, and religious among them, in which individuals' inner conflicts often play as large a role as do the external factors. This is a loosely defined group which includes a wide range of titles. They are: *All This, And Heaven Too, My Sister Eileen, The Best of Damon Runyon, Oliver Wiswell, Random Harvest, Dragon Seed, Damon Runyon Favorites, So Little Time, The Human Comedy, Green Dolphin Street, The Razor's Edge, Forever Amber, So Well Remembered, Cass Timberlane,* and *Claudia.*

Four of the remaining books can be classed together as psychological studies of a person afflicted with some curse and their effect on those around them. In *Rebecca* the title character's curse is responsible for the motion of the plot. Rebecca's wickedness and her husband's consequent murder of her form a secret which is the curse on his second wife. In *Strange Woman* the leading lady, Jenny Hager, poisons all she touches. The same is true of Ellen Bernet in *Leave Her to Heaven.* Her extreme possessiveness leads her to great destruction and even murder. A similar result occurs from Nicholas Van Ryn's monomaniacal desire for a son in *Dragonwyck.* In all but *Rebecca* a rational good finally prevails over the curse.

The three remaining books are children's books, dealing with animals. They are: *The Yearling, Lassie-Come-Home,* and *My Friend Flicka.* All three stress the child's role as a part of a family and the fact that his acceptance of duty and virtue leads to rewards. They also involve fairly complicated choices which the young children have to make. This follows the general trend towards recognition of complexity.

The books thus are varied, subtle and intricate. They speak for a period even more varied and even more complex. During World War II, unlike the period of World War I, the thought about the war reflected in best sellers preceded and accompanied the great action of the war rather than appearing primarily afterwards as a critique of the fighting and its horrors. Three basic causes for the new type of thought and expression can be given: first, a delayed reaction to the Depression and sizable recognition of the overall social responsibility it demanded; second, recognition of the horror of Nazism, and acceptance of the responsibility for eradicating it; and, third, the more open, more fluid society created by the war.

These three factors are primarily responsible for the new trends in 1938 and afterwards. Yet there is also a fourth, a silent, factor. It is a factor of age. It is a result of the time lapse since the personal revolution of the twenties. Gradually, through the adolescent revolution of the twenties, and through a fear-inspired set-back of the thirties, America had truly come of age. This period most thoroughly represents the end of American innocence.[1]

The fifty books were written by forty-three different authors. Thirty-five of the authors were appearing on the best seller list for the first time. In other words, fewer authors in this group were known to a large part of the reading public because of their earlier books. The authors were born during the period 1874 to 1919, from three years earlier to fourteen years later than those writing during the previous period. At the time of publication, they ranged in age from 26 to 70, clearly a wide age span. The authors' birthplaces are also varied, but the majority came from the Northeast (13) and from foreign countries (17). This is the most impressive number of foreigners of all periods except 1918-1927 which had ten books out of twenty-seven written by foreign authors. The regions of this country outside the Northeast are underrepresented. Seven of the authors came from the Middle West, five from the West, and three from the South.

The fifty books included makes this the largest of the groups. The mysteries, with forty-two, were second in number and, as has been pointed out, most of those were read during this time period. Of the fifty books, twenty-four were over 400 pages in length. The trend towards long books begun in the early thirties had continued. Obviously, more people were reading more. Historical novels also remained popular. Fourteen of the fifty books are historical novels. The rest are contemporary, or they take place earlier in the twentieth century.

Not surprisingly, thirty-two of the stories take place partially or completely in foreign countries. This marks a continuation of the trend begun during the twenties and thirties. Of the American locales, fourteen include the Northeast, only two include the South, five the middle West, and five the Far West. This is a change away from the closer geographical balance of the thirties and, to an only slightly lesser extent, the twenties. The locales during the period 1938 to 1945 are fairly evenly divided between cities and towns. Very few have rural settings. It must be noted that the majority of the cities are American and the majority of the towns are European. The settings are as varied as were those of the twenties, but now there is not a consciousness that they are particularly exotic.

Stylistically, this group of books is characterized by straightforward although not overly simplistic linguistic presentation. Colloquial language, regional dialects and foreign phrases appear in roughly one-sixth of the books. Class dialects appear in fifteen of the fifty. These figures mark no great change from the thirties.

There is some element of humor in most of these books, but it is usually small. Most of the humor comes through comic day-to-day interaction. Despite the strong criticism of unreformed prejudices and irresponsibilities, humor does not become a weapon of attack as it was during the twenties. The forties resembles the thirties in that the books present serious questions seriously. They do, however, lack the self-righteous quality of many of the Depression novels.

Part of the emergence into the modern world was the recognition of the importance of the political process. Compared with all the other periods, interest in politics rates very high from 1938 to 1945. In the end, the view of politics presented reveals a gradual acceptance of the New Deal and the recognition that America, as the world's strongest nation industrially, had responsibility to fight the evil of the German National Socialists.

As the large number of war-centered stories would indicate, most of the books treating international political questions are concerned with World War II. There are a few references to international politics of other periods, generally distant wars viewed from the present.

The majority of the books about World War II involve participation in fighting for the just cause. Many young men leave to go to war. In *Earth and High Heaven*, Marc Reiser leaves his new wife to fight, and she agrees that he must. In Alice Duer Miller's *The White Cliffs*, American Susan allows her British son Percy to follow in his father's footsteps in the continuing generation of Englishmen who are willing to die for England. In James Ramsey Ullman's *The White Tower*, Mark Ordway, an American pilot who had been shot down leaves the haven of Switzerland to return to the fight. Often this going off to the physical fight is incidental to a more central element of the plot, but in John Steinbeck's *The Moon Is Down* it forms the main theme of the plot. The whole Norwegian town joins in resisting the Germans despite threats of all kinds of retaliation. The Norwegian mayor explains to the Germans that his townspeople wiil fight to the end for their freedom and that, in the end, they will win:

Free men cannot start a war, but once it is started, they can fight on in defeat.

> Herd men, followers of a leader, cannot do that, and so it is always the herd men who win battles and the free men who win wars.[2]

At the end of the book, Mayor Orden refuses to tell his townspeople to stop their resistance even though his life is the price of the next bombing.

This sort of solidarity is typical of these novels. The earlier ones, concerning England's plight, show English bravery in such a way that Americans would feel encouraged to help. Pearl Buck's *Dragon Seed* tells how the Chinese peasants were encouraged in their resistance to the Japanese when they heard that the great white nations were fighting the same enemy.

The unanimity of the books is interesting. Although there are regrets that wars must be fought, the cause is never questioned. Even in Hemingway's *For Whom the Bell Tolls*, about the struggle in Spain which preceded World War II, Robert Jordan's participation against the fascists is never questioned.

Any opposition is to war in general, never in terms of an assertion that the Nazis should be supported. Mrs. Miniver clings to the everyday human things that continue eternally despite wars. In *Oliver Wiswell*, about the American Revolution, Kenneth Roberts shows the tragedy of war in terms of the lives of all the individuals involved. Roberts' book, however, is one of those left-overs from the thirties which view the Revolution and democracy with suspicion blaming the demagoguery of Sam Adams. The only expression of the idea that World War II was senseless came from the German Colonel Lanser in *The Moon Is Down* who hates the cruelties of war and who sees beyond army organization to the feelings of the individual soldiers. Steinbeck holds out a hope of a better world in the humanity he attributes to the German common soldiers:

> Their talk was of friends and relatives who loved them and their longings were for warmth and love, because a man can be a soldier for only so many hours a day and for only so many months in a year, and then he wants to be a man again, wants girls and drinks and music and laughter and ease. . . .[3]

This concern with basic humanity and living is reflected in other ways also. In *So Little Time*, John Marquand has Jeffrey Wilson wanting his son Jim to live all the life he can because soon he will have to go to war amd may be killed.

In William Saroyan's *The Human Comedy*, good people are killed because of the war and that, of course, saddens the characters, but the war is shown as bringing consciousness too. Young Homer has gone to work as a telegraph delivery boy because his family needs the money. One night after delivering another War Department message of death, Homer cries in his sleep. His mother, Kate, a Mother Earth type like Ma Joad in *The Grapes of Wrath*, comforts him:

> I know that sobbing . . . I have heard it before. It is not yours. It is not any man's. It is the whole world's. Having known the world's grief, you are now on your way. . . . Many times you will laugh and many times you will weep, but always you will laugh and weep together. You will never have a moment of time in your life to be mean or petty or small.[4]

This is a parallel between the maturing of the young boy Homer and the maturing of America.

By the last years of the war, Americans had not only accepted their responsibility in fighting but were also beginning to consider what the world would be like after the war. In *A Bell for Adano*, the men of the occupation army in Italy recognized how much influence the men in control can have over the happiness and well-being of the common people. Major Joppolo was in charge of the American forces in an Italian town. Author John Hersey wrote in his preface:

> Major Victor Joppolo, U. S. A., was a good man. You will see that. It is the whole reason why I want you to know his story.[5]

Joppolo does a very effective job in Adano. He gets the town on its feet after the wartime disintegration and even instills some of the better practices of democracy into popular favor. He tells the townspeople his goals:

> I want you to be happy together. I want all of you to have as much as you can of what you want, without hurting anyone else. That is what I want in Adano.[6]

Joppolo however is thwarted in his efforts. Some local carts have slowed down the car of a general called Marvin when he is on his way through the town. Despite the fact that the carts are an economic necessity, Marvin orders them banned from the town. When Joppolo does not enforce this, Marvin has him removed. The point of the book is the contrast between what good can be done by good men in control and what harm can be done by bad men in control. There is a rather unconcealed plea to put the power in the hands of the good men.

Many of these books do have a sort of propaganda point to make. The fact that political questions are considered important enough to warrant pleading is an innovation. All of the books accept America's active role in World War II. A few, like *A Bell for Adano*, imply the necessity of a continuing active role. War generally is viewed as bad but necessary, involvement in international politics simply as necessary. Heroic achievement, especially in war, is praised.

Domestic national politics is not central to any of the novels in the same way that the war is. There is, however, much more interest in national politics than there has been previously. The explanation of one of the minor characters in *The Human Comedy* was that the war had led to a generalized interest in politics. This is only partially true. The early novels from the early part of this period reveal a strong interest in that question raised by the New Deal—what is the position of the economic lower class—and the books show a sympathy for those people rather than for the rich. With the exception of *Oliver Wiswell*, in which the characters are mostly Loyalists in the American Revolution, most characters involved in domestic political questions take the liberal side.

In Rachel Field's *All This, And Heaven Too*, the leading lady, Henriette, is on the republican side in the French Revolution. The debate between Henriette and the Duke she loves puts the issue as the good life for the little people versus order. Symptomatically, the Duke considers Americans savages and Henriette judges them to be the true republicans who may change the world. However, none of the differences in opinion are strong enough to prevent the two from falling in love.

Another novel with a non-American setting makes a plea for purity in government and for a government that will take care of the masses of people. In *The Robe* by Lloyd Douglas, Roman Senator Galio talks to his son Marcellus:

> . . . we could use a few men in the Roman Senate with the brains and bravery of your slave, Demetrius. . . . One day the slaves are going to take over this rotted government! . . . It lacks cohesion. But some day it will develop a leader, a cause, a slogan, a banner. Three-fourths of this city's inhabitants either have been or are slaves. . . . It would require a very shrewd and powerful Government to keep in subjugation three times its size and strength. But–look at our Government! A mere hollow shell! It has no moral fiber! Content with its luxury, indolence, and profligacy, its extravagant pageants in honor of its silly gods; ruled by an insane dotard and a drunken nonentity! So, my son, Rome is doomed![7]

Lloyd Douglas comments further on the injustice of that government which lets the rich get around morality and the law while the poor must abide by them. This same point is made by Samuel Shellabarger in *Captain From Castile* where a dancer at a country inn comments: "The law protects people who are born in big beds."[8] In nearly all of the books, the readers' sympathies are to be with the unprivileged.

The greatest acceptance of the need for politically induced economic change is indicated in books which show the plight of the groups helped by the reform legislation. Several examples will illustrate. The case for the economic lower classes is most strongly presented by the Welsh author Richard Llewellyn in *How Green Was My Valley* and by John Steinbeck in *The Grapes of Wrath*, but these are by no means the only books that consider such problems.

How Green Was My Valley takes place in a Welsh mining town. First the poverty and hardship of the miners' lives is shown. There are mine accidents which kill some men and leave others permanently incapable of working. Those latter receive no pension. The brothers of the young boy narrator lead strikes for higher wages. Eventually the owners lower wages and inflict even greater hardships. The negative role of the government is criticized. Acceptance by the readers of this criticism implies an acceptance of New Deal support for labor organization and the establishment of better living conditions for workers.

In *The Grapes of Wrath* also there is little direct comment on the Federal Government. Instead, Steinbeck describes the plight of the share-croppers as they must leave their homes, live sometimes in tents, face police brutality and near starvation.

Probably the most valuable function of this book was to make the croppers human individuals to a group of readers who previously had seen them merely as the mass poor, dirty and ignorant. The obsolete middle class view is illustrated by a conversation by two men in a gas station where the Joads stop:

> "Jesus, what a hard-looking outfit!"
> "Them Okies? They're all hard-lookin'."
> "Jesus, I'd hate to start out in a jalopy like that."
> "Well, you and me got sense. Them goddamn Okies got no sense and no feeling. They ain't human. A human being wouldn't live like they do. A human being couldn't stand it to be so dirty and miserable. They ain't a hell of a lot better than gorillas."
> "Just the same I'm glad I ain't crossing the desert in no Hudson Super-Six. She sounds like a threshing machine."
> The other boy looked down at his book of bills. And a big drop of sweat rolled down his finger and fell on the pink bills. "You know, they don't have much trouble. They're so goddamn dumb they don't know it's dangerous. And, Christ Almighty, they don't know any better than what they got. Why worry?"[9]

There are other examples. The only similar presentation to come before this period was *God's Little Acre.*

As the Depression drew to a close, people began to recognize the problems it presented and, implicitly, the need for the solution provided by the Federal Government. Significantly, this recognition came largely after the reading group were no longer threatened. Throughout this period, it must be noted, there is no basic challenge to the American system. Even Robert Jordan, in *For Whom the Bell Tolls*, who is fighting on the liberal side in the Spanish Civil War, supports the American system of breaking up the big estates by taxes rather than by revolution as the Spanish were attempting to do. The desire, obviously, is to perfect the American system, to make it fulfill its ideals, not to destroy it.

Presentations of local politics and local governments very much resemble the presentation of the same on a national level. The emphasis is on the relation of the local government to the poorer economic classes. In James Hilton's *So Well Remembered*, George Boswell is considered a good mayor because he looks out for the interests of the lower classes first. He sponsors such undertakings as housing projects to replace slums. In *A Bell for Adano*, Major Joppolo provided an example of what a good mayor should do.

Several books have as a chief local issue the ownership of the land. In *The Black Rose* by Thomas B. Costain, one of the heroes of the adventure in the Far East, Tristram Griffen leads a revolt against the local landowners. He explains his undertaking:

> We have learned many things through the long centuries—one thing above all else: that the land belongs to everyone and not to the few. Some men become rich while most remain poor; but the land must be so used that there will be food for every belly.[10]

Tris receives some support in the effort at land reform from the king. In the end, however, he is martyred to the cause. In *Dragonwyck*, Anya Seton describes a similar land revolt, this time by the small farmers against the Hudson Valley aristocracy. In one book, Rosamond Marshall's *Kitty*, the owner of a large estate initiates reform. Kitty closes down the sweatshops in her village, cleans up the town, and builds a school for the children of her workers. As a result, her village is burnt down.

Another sort of plea for reform based on a local observation is made by Mrs. Miniver. She observes the changes in her town after the beginning of World War II and comments:

> . . . it oughtn't to *need* a war to make a nation paint its kerbstones white, carry rear-lamps on its bicycles, and give all its slum children a holiday in the country. . . . However, it *has* needed one: which is about the severest criticism our civilization could have.[11]

Mrs. Miniver has generalized from the local to the national.

Not only is there a book about a mayor who helps the lower classes, but there is also one about a governor. In *A Lion Is In the Streets*, Adria Locke Langley gives a fictionalized account of the career of Huey Long. Despite his corruption and megolomania, the book shows the plight of the poor whites and what Hank Martin (Huey) does to help them to build roads to open up markets so the farmers can get fair prices, to build better schools, and to provide free text books. For this, the people love him, despite all his corruption.

As is by now clear, the local and national political issues appear irrevocably connected. The same problems are treated in both contexts and the solution offered is the same: government responsibility for the lower economic classes and broad economic reform. This is a far cry from the Depression-time assertion of the ideal of the independent hard-worker who can always make it if he tries. Finally this is a recognition that individuals cannot always control their own destiny and that some greater power must take the responsibility.

The war, and the accompanying assumption of world responsibility, and the concern for the status of the economically deprived groups in society both mark complete changes from *all* the earlier periods. The cosmopolitanism of the twenties is here but has been expanded to include an institutional political character as well as that necessary prerequisite, the interest in the individuals. The twenties and the thirties marked the beginning of acceptance of and concern for individuals of different nationalities and different income groups within America. The novels of this period 1938 to 1945 provide the logical next step: the concern with those people as a whole, realizing that the fate of the whole affected that of each individual.

In these same years ethnic discrimination and conflict became a matter of serious concern in American best sellers. Several of the books make this their central problem, and many others include ethnic considerations to an important extent. Race is of at least contributing importance in twelve of the books and enters in in a more minor way in twenty-four more. This interest itself is a change from the twenties and thirties. The books continue the pattern begun in the twenties and lost in the thirties of accepting individuals for themselves but often carry that further to a more general concern.

Given the normal rate of carry-over of the attitude of the previous period, amazingly few of the books in this group accept racial prejudice. Several of the comments in *The Black Rose* carry the reminder of the earlier period. Walter of Gurnie and his set at Oxford obviously considered Jews different. He describes one part of his dormitory life:

> The Hall backs on the Jewry, and it's a favorite evening pastime with some of our fellows to watch the girls through the glass without their plackerds on.[12]

Once in the East Walter and Tris rescue a girl who is half English, half Eastern. They consider her especially worth rescuing from a

Mongul harem because of her English blood. Walter comments on the Monguls:

> These Monguls are not human—not as we understand human nature. They live by a code called the Ulang-Yassa. It teaches them they are a superior race, that it's their duty to despise, deceive, cheat, and kill all other people.[13]

This is the only book in which racial stereotyping is both important and is done by a leading non-villain character. It is also the only book in which proposals for economic reform and derogatory racial stereotyping exist together and where both are of major importance. It should be noted that the discussions of race take place near the beginning of the book and the drive for land reform takes place at the end.

Most of the books reject racial stereotyping. In *Escape*, the German characters sometimes try to assert their superiority. This assertion of superiority is rejected by the other characters in this and all other books. In *The Moon Is Down* Steinbeck rejects the stereotyping of Germans as do the authors of several books. A few of the books have characters who are anti-Semitic, but these usually are put down in the same manner. In *So Little Time*, a friend tells Jeff Wilson who works in the theater: "You're too good to waste your time working for a bunch of Jews in Hollywood."[14] Jeff, however, rejects his friend's attitude. The strongest plea against anti-Semitism occurs in Gwethalyn Graham's *Earth and High Heaven* where the plot centers on the love between a young Jewish lawyer Marc Reiser and the daughter of a socially prominent family in Montreal, Erica Drake. For a while, her parents will not have him in the house. His parents, with similar stereotyping of the goyim, think little more of the romance. The extent of the personal hurt is shown. The Jewish stereotype is challenged by making Marc's brother David a country doctor who loves the woods and often treats people without pay. Marc wants to practice law in a small town because those people need the skill more than the richer city people do. Finally, the question lying behind the whole period is asked openly: is the war being fought to protect the old values, including social prejudice and stratification, or is it to bring a new and better system? The younger generation obviously chooses the latter. And, when they assert themselves, they win. In another book, *Kitty Foyle*,

Christopher Morley makes the point in a slightly different way. Kitty, after being rejected by Philadelphia socialite Wynnewood Straffort, VI, because he does not have the strength to resist his parents, goes out with a Jew, Marcus Eisen. She speaks forthrightly:

> I'd be a better American if I married Mark than if I'd married Wyn. The more we get mixed up, I mean race-mixed-up, the better.[15]

This same tendency against discrimination, perhaps made especially conscious because of the Nazis' treatment of Jews, is carried over to other racial groups: Orientals, European immigrant groups, and Negroes. Several examples for each group illustrate the trend.

In *The Keys of the Kingdom*, A. J. Cronin tells about a Catholic priest who serves for many years as a missionary in China. In this book, all the sensitive people treat the Chinese like other human beings. Only the ignorant consider them backward. In Pearl Buck's *Dragon Seed* the Chinese are, of course, admirable. Here many consider the white skinned foreigners funny, but they too can prove themselves.

Marcia Davenport's *The Valley of Decision* deals with the status of immigrants more forthrightly than any other book in all the novels considered. The story takes place in Pittsburgh over the period from 1873 to 1941. It is long enough for several different immigrant groups to appear on the scene. The heroine of the story is Mary Rafferty. At the beginning of the book she is a sixteen-year-old Irish immigrant house maid. She and one of the family sons fall in love. She refuses to marry him because of her inferior status. This is shown as a tragedy and the reader is meant to disagree with her reasoning. The man continues to love her throughout his whole life. The next group of immigrants to arrive are the Slavs. Mary befriends a Czech family named Liska. They work hard and become citizens. Mary and others like her fight to have all these people be accepted as equal members of society. By the end of the story, the younger generation and the newer ideas are winning out and members of the old families are willing to marry Slavs, accepting individuals as such.

John Hersey speaks for the new fighters for toleration in his preface to *A Bell for Adano*. He enunciates once more the melting pot ideal:

America is the international country. Major Joppolo was an Italian-American going to work in Italy. Our Army has Yugoslavs and Frenchmen and Austrians and Czechs and Norwegians in it, and everywhere our Army goes in Europe, a man can turn to the private beside him and say: "Hey, Mac, what's this furriner saying? How much does he want for that bunch of grapes?" And Mac will be able to translate.[16]

For Hersey, and presumably for some of his readers, the collection of people with different national backgrounds is no longer a cause for worry but is instead an asset.

There is not such a unanimous victory for equal status for Negroes, but in these best sellers their position is improved. Three books illustrate the range of the variety. In *A Lion Is In the Streets*, the Negroes presented fit into Southern stereotype. They are less bright, but loyal and sensitive. A Negro dialect is written in. Hank explains, when he is running for office, that he does not want any black votes because any Negro allegiance would drive away the poor white vote on which he was relying. His stand is that of a political realist rather than that of a racist. He does make a point of explaining that the economic benefits he hopes to gain for the poor whites will benefit the poor blacks too.

Kitty Foyle, despite her integrationist attitude towards Jews, does single out Negroes for racial stereotyping. The qualities she attributes are good, but it is still stereotyping. She says:

Colored people don't have to stop and think in order to be wise; they just know about things naturally, it oozes out of them.[17]

On the other hand, she agrees with her father when he says Negroes are just as clean as white people and therefore should be allowed to use the same toilets. Obviously, discussion of racial matters is becoming more open and more elementary.

The fullest treatment given to the status of Negroes and the relationship between whites and Negroes occurs in Lillian Smith's novel *Strange Fruit.* The fruit is a lynched body swinging in the breeze. The plot centers around a love affair between mulatto Nonnie Anderson and white Tracy Deen. The action takes place in a small Southern town, allowing most of the leading citizens, both black and white, to appear. The tragedy and hurt and shame heaped on the Negroes is made vivid by all that happens in the town of Maxwell. Nonnie, beautiful and sensitive and college-educated, can find a job only as a nursemaid. The Negro physician, Dr. Sam Perry, is called Sam by all the whites. He puts up with it, because if he did not he would no longer be allowed to practice medicine. The local preacher provides an example of Christian love for all men when he lectures Tracy trying to convince him to marry the white girl his family wants him to.

This world's full of young folks wanting—strange things. That's youth and the devil . . . and sooner or later you have to face it. Funny thing . . . once you make up your mind to leave colored women alone and stick to your own kind, you soon get weaned.[18]

Tracy obviously does not agree with Preacher Dunwoodie's implication that all black women are alike and that their appeal is animalistic. For a long while, he and Nonnie, whose family also objects, are ready to fight the world. When she gets pregnant, they talk about getting married and going to France. Social pressures win out over love though, and Tracy leaves Nonnie who has decided to have the baby anyway. When her brother discovers that Tracy is the father, he kills him. It is the ultimate weapon, but also the only one available to a black man. The whites then must revenge white blood with black and lynch a retarded Negro named Big Henry, whom they know is innocent. The point of the book is particularly poignant because the author creates an atmosphere of admiration and hope for the lovers who dare to go against social convention. They dare to dream, but then Tracy loses his courage and destroys the dream for them both. The guilty party is white racism. This book represents the extreme of closeness and love between individuals of different races. Furthermore it places the most severe criticism on the white man's prejudice.

Just as the thirties brought a decrease in ethnic toleration and in the willingness of the readers to accept members of other economic classes, the forties brought an increase in both. In the novels that sold the best from 1938 to 1945, lower class characters are featured prominently in twenty-five of the fifty. This is the highest percentage of any group. This figure is contrasted to the number of twenty-three books where upper-class characters appear in important roles and thirty-two where middle-class characters do. The middle class still predominates, but not by a very wide margin. Despite the protest on behalf of the lower classes, faith in the capitalist system continued. In 1940 and afterwards, fifteen of the books include at least one significant example of movement upward on the economic scale. Only six books include equally important examples of declining economic status. Although most of the authors assert the equal humanity and therefore rights of all classes, the majority of the books show some sort of antagonism between the classes. The second most prevalent attitude is that of members of the upper and middle classes who want to help their less fortunate fellow citizens.

After the issues of reform and why it is necessary, the second important economic point made in these novels is similar to one made earlier, that is that money should not be considered of great importance. Certainly many of the characters in the novels of these years are well off financially, but many other characters protest against money as either unnecessary or evil. A number of characters are fascinating despite their lack of money. Cluny Brown is an English maid. After numerous adventures she marries Adam Belinski, a Polish intellectual. Francie Nolan and her whole family in Betty Smith's *A Tree Grows in Brooklyn* are poor Irish but good people. The author points out how middle class prejudice works to keep the poor from rising. In school Francie, who is smart, has problems with her teachers who favor the richer, cleaner children. Francie, believing in the American dream, puts herself through school and rises economically. Her goodness correlates with neither economic status. They are unconnected. Damon Runyon in the compilation of stories created a whole world of comparatively unmonied characters who are fascinating. The poor thus are not only impoverished, usually in need of help, but also interesting individuals.

Other books show the pointlessness of the pursuit of money when other, more valuable elements in life are lacking. This point is similar to the idea presented in the novels of the twenties when money is valued only as a means to exciting living and also to the disdain of money in the absence of spiritual values presented in the novels of the thirties. *The Razor's Edge* by Somerset Maugham presents a point of view closer to that of the thirties. Isabel Bradley Maturin cannot bring herself to marry Larry Darrell, her true love, because he does not have much money. She eventually gains financial security but she never attains happiness. Larry, on the other hand, achieves contentment. In Marquand's *So*

Little Time, Jeffrey Wilson comments on his wife's society-minded friends. He says they live their empty lives in their fancy houses "like playing dolls."[19]

Two books make explicit statements. In *The Human Comedy* Marcus describes his father as a great man:

> We're poor, always have been—my father was a *great* man. He was not a successful man. He didn't make any more money than we needed—ever. . . . The only thing he cared about was his family.[20]

The human values prevail here. This is not a criticism of money but an assertion that other personal values are more important. In *For Whom the Bell Tolls* there is a direct assertion that property corrupts. Robert Jordan speaks of what happened to Pablo, one of the guerillas, who acquired some horses:

> The horses made him rich and as soon as he was rich he wanted to enjoy life. Pretty soon he'll feel bad because he can't join the Jockey Club. . . .[21]

Despite this comment, however, most of the lower class characters and their creators believe that all should share in the distirubtion of worldly goods rather than spurn them. Kitty from Rosamond Marshall's book expresses it one way. She has risen from the streets.

> I want there should not be one crimphouse, or one brothy in all the world. I want there should be plenty of soap, like the piece I washed with here! And especially I want there should be bread for empty bellies. It's the fear of hunger that makes bawdies and beggars and thieves![22]

Many people, like Kitty, express the desire that all might rise. On the other hand, middle class characters and monied characters in general are no longer defensive about their status as they were during the thirties.

One marked change from the thirties is that no profession is predominant among the good characters. Like the heroes of the twenties, their occupations vary widely. Artists, farmers, maids, noblemen, miners, writers, priests, businessmen, housewives, politicians and students and some others are all represented. In books where there are villains, they tend to be soldiers, often but not always of the Axis powers, and rich businessmen and owners. Not surprisingly, the occupation and the achievement of success at it are both of major importance in only twelve of the books. The nature of the occupation and the achievement of success at an occupation bear almost exactly the same importance for the whole group of novels. It is successful achievement rather than the mere accumulation of money which is judged good. It would thus appear that the society is more achievement oriented than it is status oriented. Or, to express it differently, status is gained by personal achievement not by mere possession of wealth. This is generally true for all periods studied.

As a great virtue, work has declined from the thirties. It is of major importance in only eight of the novels of this group. Diligence is not attacked to any great extent. The fact is simply that the whole defensive reassertion of the Horatio Alger myth disappeared with the end of the Depression. Native skill, which implies a natural elite, is considered very important in fifteen of the novels of this group. Except for the novels of the thirties, skill is generally much more important than hard work. Skill is almost always necessary for success. Hard work is necessary only sometimes. The most haunting image of the desire for achievement which requires skill is that of Jeffrey Wilson in *So Little Time* giving up his mistress Marianna Miller saying the romance is not right because even it has not given him the inspiration to write a great play. Skill is more important than hard work in all the groups of books, even in those of the thirties. For some reason, readers still chose to read about characters who do belong to one elite or another. This is true in this period, as it was in others, despite the assertion that all members of society deserve a portion of its natural benefits.

Formal education is not so important in this group of books as it was in the thirties. Here no special point is made of the role of education. The characters generally consider education good but, with the exception of Hank Martin in *A Lion Is In the Streets,* no great struggle to gain education plays a central role.

Art has remained of comparatively little importance after 1938, but it is not as completely ignored as it was during the Depression. There are numerous instances of an art form being meaningful to someone. Jeffrey Wilson longs to write his play. In Sinclair Lewis' *Cass Timberlane*, Jinny seeks after art in her small Middle Western town. In *A Bell for Adano* Major Joppolo works hard to obtain a bell for the town because the people love its music. In *The Valley of Decision* the son of a Czech immigrant worker becomes a great musician. In *A Tree Grows in Brooklyn* Francie's father, Johnnie Nolan, is an Irish singer. His music, although not great from a professional point of view, brings much beauty to her life. In *Kitty*, the artist Gainsborough plays a part in the story, and the man Kitty falls in love with she saw first in a painting of his. An art form thus has a powerful effect. Art has re-entered people's lives, but generally as an extra beauty or satisfaction, never as a central question which it sometimes was before World War I. It is now a part of the complex world.

Nature plays a more frequent role than art does. Some consideration of the natural world enters in to twenty-one of the novels, often in a minor fashion and five times in a fairly important way. Generally natural forces are judged to be good. Only four times does it have that saving quality that it did in the period before World War I. Several times it is threatening. The biggest threat from the natural order is described by Marjorie Kennan Rawlings in *The Yearling*. It is the yearling's nature to eat the crops that grow. When he eats the Baxter family's crops, which provide their means of livelihood, he must be shot. In *The White Tower* nature, while dangerous, is basically to be conquered. Most of the characters in the story hope to scale the steep mountain called Weissturm. Lassie also conquers nature to return to the boy she loves.

Most often, however, nature is judged good and beautiful. In Elizabeth Goudge's *Green Dolphin Street*, William Ozanne loves the wild country of New Zealand. In *Earth and High Heaven*, Graham uses the Jewish characters' love of nature to show how sensitive they are. In *A Tree Grows in Brooklyn* Francie cherishes the one little tree by her house. In *The Valley of Decision* there is a flood which nearly drowns the two lovers but it gives them a chance to be alone together, and they are glad. In Mary O'Hara's *My Friend Flicka* everyone loves the pure air of the West. There is some indication that the country makes women better women and best teaches boys to be men.

The Grapes of Wrath contains the most poetic description of the close relationship between the land and man. Together they live; when separated they both die. The people love the land they farm, and the land is vacant and dead without men. Steinbeck describes what is left after the owners have forced the croppers off the land:

> The houses were left vacant on the land, and the land was vacant because of this. Only the tractor sheds of corrugated iron, silver and gleaming, were alive; and they were alive with metal and gasoline and oil, the disks of the plows shining. The tractors had lights shining, for there is no day and night for a tractor and the disks turn the earth in the darkness and they glitter in the daylight. And when a horse stops work and goes into the barn there is a life and a vitality left, there is a breathing and a warmth, and the feet shift on the straw, and the jaws clamp on the hay, and the ears and the eyes are alive. There is a warmth of life in the barn, and the heat and smell of life. But when the motor of a tractor stops, it is as dead as the ore it came from. The heat goes out of it like the living heat that leaves a corpse. . . . [The tractor is] so easy that the wonder goes out of work, so efficient that the wonder goes out of land and the working of it, and with the wonder the deep understanding and the relation.[23]

In this period then, best sellers tended to depict man and nature in harmony. In some of the stories nature plays an important role. However, the natural world never provides a key to salvation as it did before World War I. Again, in the complex world, it has however regained a role.

In conclusion, the most important changes in points of view about the world outside the individual occur in the areas of political and ethnic concerns. The political viewpoint expressed in the novels has developed in several significant ways. Internationally, there is a general commitment to American participation in World War II and its fight in a just cause. Furthermore, several books, like *A Bell for Adano*, indicate a recognition of the fact that our international responsibility would continue after the war's end. In the area of domestic politics the authors express a similar recognition of responsibility. In this case, it is the responsibility of society in general for the economically deprived. Furthermore, a majority of the books that concern themselves with this indicate that the government, national and local, must act for society to bring about politically induced economic change. The poor are now presented both as fully portrayed individuals and as a group in need.

The novels of this group reveal a similar widening of horizons in treatment of ethnic considerations. Racial stereotyping is consciously refuted in a number of the books. The emphasis on the goodness of many Jewish characters shows clearly the strength of the reaction to Nazism. But the same treatment is also applied to various hyphenated Americans, Orientals, and in a few cases to Negroes. The only stereotypes still put forward strongly are of Negroes, but the appearance of a book like *Strange Fruit* provides an indication that a change in attitudes is beginning here, too.

One might infer from these facts not only an increasing sense of political, economic and social responsibilities, but also a determination to make real the ideals that men were fighting for in World War II. In addition to this determination, there was a recognition of the complexity of reality which precluded the proposing of over-simplified solutions.

Family relations, like the rest of the characteristics of this period, are varied. They are of major importance in twenty-nine of the fifty books. They are of lesser importance in most of the others. They can be both good and bad. When the stories are finished, more families are living in harmony than not. When things do not end well, they almost always end in coldness rather than in active conflict. The lack of self-conscious rebellion continues from the thirties. Where there are family disagreements, there is often a specific point at issue rather than simply independence.

Children-parent relationships take on two basic forms: either harmony or rupture for a specific reason. In *Strange Fruit* the fight is between Tracy Deen and his parents over his relationship with a black girl. In *How Green Was My Valley* the Morgan sons break with their father when they want to organize a miners' union and he opposes it. In *Earth and High Heaven* the issue is whether the daughter of a society family should marry a Jew. She does. The issues that bring rupture thus are precisely the ones which represent the changes in social outlook from the earlier periods.

More often, harmony prevails. Several examples will serve as sufficient illustration. In *Lassie-Come-Home*, when Lassie is missing:

Joe Carraclough solved his problem as hundreds of thousands of boys solve their problems the world over. He ran home to tell his mother.[24]

Mrs. Miniver repeatedly glorifies her life as wife and mother, as do several other women.

In several families, the parents are contrasted to each other in terms of their effect on their children. In *The Green Years*, Mr. and Mrs. Leckie have forgotten about loving their children in their over-concern for money. But Grandpa knows about happiness and provides that element in young Robie's life. In *The Yearling*, Ma Baxter enforces strictness, but Pa Baxter believes Jody should have a chance to be a boy. In *Lassie-Come-Home*, Joe and his father Sam share a men's secret: that they must tolerate Mrs. Carraclough's yelling and scolding sometimes because women must stay in the house and so they take things out somehow. Very few of the books express the sort of attitude left over from the twenties as does Ruth McKenney in *My Sister Eileen* where she makes the mother a nonentity and the father appear silly. As these examples illustrate, some individual relationships between parents and their children are interesting but, as a group, they represent no special pattern of change. The only new trend is the tendency to break over the newly found social conscience of the younger generation.

Husbands and wives have similarly varied relationships, also without great changes from those in the novels of earlier periods. More of the interesting relationships are unhappy marriages. In *Dragonwyck* Nicholas Van Ryn kills his wife with oleander leaves because she does not bear him a son. In *Green Dolphin Street*, William Ozanne fell in love with one sister and married the other because he got their names mixed up when he wrote their father for permission after ten years of being held prisoner at sea. In *Claudia*, Rose Franken presents a young wife who loved housekeeping for the first few years and then who began to wonder if she still had any sex appeal and so picked up a writer who had moved into town. Her marriage prevails, however, and happily. In James Hilton's *So Well Remembered*, Livia Boswell left her husband, the man who became mayor of Browdley, to marry a man with more money. In *Leave Her to Heaven*, Ben Ames Williams describes the strangest relationship between any wife and husband in any of these best sellers. Ellen Berent Harland in order to obtain complete possession of her husband Richard has let his crippled brother Danny drown. The marriage became cold, but Richard would not turn her in. After she dies, he finally goes to jail for his failure to report the crime. He provides the explanation:

> She was his wife, and between man and wife there was a bond which never could be broken. He might condemn her utterly—and love and defend her still.[25]

The most interesting marital relationship takes place in Marquand's *So Little Time.* Here the situation is most fully discussed. Madge Wilson is interested in maintaining her position in society. Jeff is looking for emotional satisfaction which social conventions do not provide. Jeff has always wanted to write a great play. He never has succeeded. He feels his life is hollow and meaningless. He meets an actress, Marianna Miller, who arouses him. They have an affair. But his terms for continuing it are that it allow him to be creative which he believes his marriage has stifled. When he still cannot write the great play, he gives up Marianna and returns to his wife. He does this because his role as husband and father is the only role in which he is necessary. The book concludes that the basic human need is to be needed.

The affairs are of the same sort as the marriages—a fairly routine variety. They lack the excited quality of those of the twenties. The easy acceptance of the moral revolution reflected in the novels of the thirties carries over to this period. Thirteen of the books contain some sort of extramarital activity among major characters. Sixteen of the books explicitly approve of extramarital affairs or equally explicitly make no moral judgment on them. Only two of the books indicate that such activity is immoral.

Heroes and villains both have affairs. In *Escape* by Ethel Vance, a Nazi general and the woman who helps the American escape are having an affair. The general has a wife. The mistress risks her love for her principles. Other characters also do this during this period. Most explicitly, many men leave their loves to go fight in the army. In *A Lion Is In the Streets,* Hank has an affair with a woman named Flamingo, but he still likes to have his wife Verity to come home to. In *Captain From Castile*, Pedro and Catana are living together without being married. When they have a baby which dies, they decide it is the will of God that they get married or quit.

Other situations that would have been considered highly irregular before World War I and probably rather daring by most readers during the twenties and thirties are now accepted with equanimity. Kitty Foyle and several other women have abortions. In *The Keys of the Kingdom*, author A. J. Cronin does not condemn Father Chisholm's cousin Nora for having an illegitimate baby. Walter of Gurnie in *The Black Rose* worries about his being illegitimate only until he learns that his father really loved his mother. In *A Bell for Adano*, Major Joppolo occasionally remarks that he should put the town's two prostitutes out of business, but he is never serious about it. In *Dragon Seed*, the local prostitutes who have always been social outcasts, save the good names of the other women by offering themselves to the invading Japanese.

Sexual descriptions have become slightly more vividly drawn during this period than they were previously. In *A Lion Is In the Streets*, Hank Martin talks about "kissin' . . . afore lovin'."[26] In *The White Tower* and *How Green Was My Valley* all but the final details of love-making are described. In *Strange Fruit* white people's inhibitions are described fully. Mrs. Deen, the mother of Tracy who does not marry Nonnie in the end, thinks all things physical are disgusting. This included her husband's leg in bed and nursing babies. The warmth of the Negro women is contrasted to Mrs. Deen. *Strange Fruit* even has a lesbian whose advances are described. *Kitty* also contains some vivid physical descriptions. When Kitty's old husband proves incapable of making love on their wedding night and departs to his own chamber, her lover comes to her. Kitty thinks:

> So often had we loved that every brush of lips, every light touch of the fingertips brought an echoing thrill. I know the shape of his virile body, he knew the curves of mine; I knew the spot where a kiss would build a fire in his veins, he knew the exact moment of my ecstacy.[27]

This sort of vividness did not occur before. *The Grapes of Wrath* also has moving physical descriptions, especially that of Rose of Sharon giving her milk to a starving man at the end of the book.

Also in *The Grapes of Wrath*, the question of the sinfulness of physical sex is raised. Reverend Jim Casy provides the answer for most of the generation:

> . . . I says to myself, "What's gnawin' you? Is it the screwin'? An' I says, "No, it's the sin. . . . Maybe it ain't a sin. Maybe it's just the way folks is. Maybe we been shippin' the hell out of ourselves for nothing'. . . . The hell with it! There ain't no sin and there ain't no virtue. There's just stuff people do. . . . And some of the things folks do is nice, and some ain't nice, but that's as far as any man got a right to say.
>
> I figgered about the Holy Sperit and the Jesus road. I figgered, maybe it's all men an' women we love; maybe that's the Holy Sperit—the human sperit—the whole she-bang. Maybe all men got one big soul ever-body's a part of. Now I sat there thinkin' it, an' all of a suddent—I knew it. I knew it so deep down that it was true, and I still know it.[28]

Sex, thus, has been accepted.

It becomes obvious that women have become quite liberated. They do essentially what they choose. Women again are strong characters. As the country recovered from the Depression, the position of women recovered from the set-back of the thirties. The best sellers now accept the women's rebellion of the twenties.

Men are central in twenty-two books, women in fifteen. In the rest, they carry equal importance. Men do remain dominant over women in the majority of books. They dominate, or are stronger, in thirty-three books, women in only nine. But now the women have a choice. Generally they do choose to be dominated. The freedom fought for during the twenties has been achieved. Women work in the majority of books. But now that the choice is assured, they want to be women and submit to men, at least in love.

One very interesting type of woman attains prominence in several of the novels of this period. That is the Mother Earth figure represented by Ma Joad in *The Grapes of Wrath* and Katy Macauley in *The Human Comedy*. Both are strong and steady women who give moral support that sustains their families through great crises. When the rest of the world falls apart, they maintain order. Ma Joad explains the steadiness to Pa Joad when he's about to give up. He says: "Seems like our life's over an' done." And she replies:

> It ain't Pa. An' that's one more thing a woman knows. I noticed that. Man,

> he lives in jerks—baby born an' a man dies, an' that's a jerk—gets a farm an' loses his farm, an' that's a jerk. Woman, it's all one flow, like a stream, little eddies, little waterfalls, but the river, it goes right on. Woman looks at it like that. We ain't gonna die out. People is goin' on—changin' a little, maybe, but goin' right on.[29]

This steadiness, more than any other quality, gives the women their strength in the books of this period.

Age distinction is not of as great an importance during this period as during some others, nor is tension between generations particularly great. More characters fall into the groups of mature adults and young pre-marrieds than any other. The chief disputes between the generations are over the social matters discussed under parent-children relations. When there is tension, youth tends to win out. The younger generation wins in twenty-two books as opposed to fourteen for the older. Most often it is a mild victory with few recriminations.

Considerable attention is given to defining youth and pointing out its leading characteristic. This varies widely. In *Earth and High Heaven* youth is portrayed as less prejudiced than the older generation. In Margery Sharp's *Cluny Brown* there is a comment that youth is self-centered. This viewpoint is not typical. More common are young people like the Norwegians in *The Moon Is Down* who fight bravely. In *The Human Comedy*, youth is a time for learning. Homer learns much from his experiences at his job in the telegraph office. In *The Sun Is My Undoing*, author Marguerite Steen makes the point that the impulsive decisions made early in life set the course for the rest of it. Matthew Flood's decision to take an African woman Sheba from another man and take her to Cuba with him leads to three generations of mixed blood and all the problems that brings. Most often, an attitude reminiscent of the twenties which was perhaps reinforced by the war, is that expressed in *The Razor's Edge*: "Jeunesse ne dure qu'un moment."[30] In *So Little Time*, Jeff wants his son Jim to live his youth as fully as he can because there may be so little time left to live. Pa Baxter in *The Yearling* expresses this in another way when thinking about how his son should live:

> Leave him kick up his heels . . . . and run away. Leave him build his flutter mills. The day'll come he'll not even care to.[31]

This idea of catching youth while it lasts is the predominant suggestion of the novels of the period.

Age is portrayed as having two main traits. In some books age brings a welcome reasonableness. In *Green Dolphin Street*, when the characters become old, they can all accept the situation caused by the mix-up of William Ozanne's marrying the wrong sister. In another book, Mrs. Miniver expresses a preference for age. She compares her forties to her thirties:

> . . . it was the difference between August and October, between the heaviness of late summer and the sparkle of early autumn, between the ending of an old phase and the beginning of a fresh one.[32]

This sort of preference for maturity is about evenly divided with the horror of age for reasons of either physical or emotional decay. Richard Myles in *Above Suspicion* declares:

> I've found the difference between twenty and thirty. . . . At twenty you never think of rheumatics or a chill in the bladder.[33]

There are several examples of older characters with more severe ailments, some of whom die. That is always sad. In *The Robe,* Marcellus notes the sadness of both physical and mental decay. At one point he remarks that it is unjust for men to have to age publicly after they have reached the height of their powers and suggests that they should vanish when they are at their height. Jeffrey Wilson in *So Little Time* best expresses the emotional regret of age:

> When you're young . . . lots of things are more serious, but when you're older, you wonder—whether anything you've done has ever been worthwhile. You can see it all about to go sour and you haven't any way to help it. . . . I keep wondering what's been the use, and exactly what I've been trying to do. I suppose I've been like everyone else, trying to build some sort of an umbrella, because I thought it would rain, and now I know that none of it's going to work.[34]

This is the saddest discovery for Jeffrey Wilson and, for some who express it, the saddest part of aging. Most characters in most of the books, however, have found more purpose in living, both in youth and in age, in this period of new commitment.

It now remains to explore the moral or religious beliefs which lie behind this new commitment, the new willingness to act and the new social attitudes. One basic factor that moves silently behind the writing of the whole period is optimism. In seventeen of the books human nature is portrayed as good. In only a few is human nature seen as less than good and then it is only mildly corrupt. The remaining majority allow both good and bad people in the world. Usually though this means people who perform good or bad acts, rather than people who have good or bad intentions. John Hersey expresses this attitude in *A Bell for Adano*:

> There were probably not any really bad men in Amgot [Allied Military Government Occupied Territory], but there were some stupid ones.[35]

In Max Brand's *Singing Guns*, the outlaw turns out to be a good guy who had unfortunate experiences in his youth.

The minority of characters who tend to be pessimistic sometimes try to do that intentionally either because they think that that sort of realism will increase their effectiveness or because they feel that it will decrease the possibility of pain. For example, in *The Sun Is My Undoing*, the leading characters, Pallas Burmester and Matthew Flood, both seem fated to a life deprived of their deepest wants. The proposed solution is that a few years of happiness make all the suffering bearable and are, really, all one may expect from life. The people here are still good in nature though. It is circumstances which lead to unhappiness, not human meanness. Where the distinction is drawn between good and bad people, the good people usually win.

Some characters such as Jeff Wilson in *So Little Time* and Larry Darrell in *The Razor's Edge* are still seeking meaning as many were during the twenties, but more people have a fairly definite idea of where they are going and what they want. Some change, usually as growth brings wisdom, while others show no important changes in character throughout their lives. The types are about evenly divided.

Religion and religious belief are of great importance in the books of this period. There is no unanimous view of religion; instead there are profound differences of opinion. Some criticize the failings of religious institutions; some are seeking the support provided by a firm belief. A few point out the bravery of living without the reassurance of religious concepts; a few still feel that formalized religion is necessary.

The positive value of religious commitment was asserted on many levels. In *A Lion Is In the Streets*, the black maid Selah tells Hank's wife Verity:

> Why, 'course there's life after death! A-course there is. Nature don't waste nothin'. . . . He didn't aim that his best work, which was humans, should be wasted. . . .[36]

This book deals with religion from its own point of view rather than that of the people it affects. The novels centered around religious themes, *The Song of Bernadette, The Robe,* and *The Nazarene*, do the same sort of thing. Yet even those contain a certain questioning of orthodoxy along with their acceptance. In *The Song of Bernadette*, most people admire the future saint for her piety. The local intellectual doubts, but not completely:

> True, I know that all gods are but the mirrored images of our own corporeal nature and that if the pelicans were to believe in a god, it would have to be a pelican. Yet is that no disproof of the being of divinity, but only a proof of the narrowness of the mortal mind limited to its own words and imaginings. Never could I have endured the thought of being eternally excluded from the cognition of God, to whom I feel myself akin in spite of all. I do not belong to you yonder who believe in a Heaven in the heavens. But neither am I to be reckoned among those dullards who believe in a heaven on earth to be provided by better laws and machines. To them I would prefer you yonder who believe in a Heaven in the heavens.[37]

In the end, however, more of the characters are interested in what happens on earth than they are in a distant heaven. Even those who accept something from religious forms usually do it for its earthly affect. In *So Little Time*, Jeff Wilson gets an emotional satisfaction from going into St. Patrick's Cathedral. He liked it because: "There was no sense of time."[38] The religious place was comforting. Another character, Robie Shannon in *The Green Years*, slips into a church in a time of crisis. Before this, he had been in rebellion against God:

> So much for this God who destroys children, murders them and breaks their hearts. There is no God, no justice upon earth. All hope has gone. Nothing remains but a blind defiance of the sky.[39]

But now, at the very end of the book, Cronin implies that there is an instinctual turning to religion:

How many times in the future this Robert Shannon will shuttle between apathy and ardour, rise and be smitten down again, we are not at liberty to predict—or how often he will make, and break, his peace with the Being towards whom all human impulses ascend. The fact remains that now uncontrollably, he feels the need of communicating the exaltation of his spirit, in the listening stillness. He feels suddenly that his prayer of gratitude will not fall into the void.[40]

These are some of the ways in which religion is accepted.

Many of the books are more concerned with the new man who is living without the help of religion. A nun, Marguerite, in *Green Dolphin Street*, expresses admiration for this new type of hero:

She saw the faithless as a man of stark courage. . . . Was he a grander figure without faith, she wondered? Was the peace of his stoicism a finer thing than the serenity of her own happy certainty?[41]

Even the religious then acknowledge and sometimes praise this new sort of man.

What then are the new definitions of God or non-God that have prompted people to turn away from organized religion or on which they base that turning away? There are two groups of anti-religious thought. One group essentially says that the bother is too great for the reward. The other makes positive criticisms of religious beliefs and practices and their effects.

In the group that simply pass religion off as not worthwhile fall the books which poke fun at religious traditions. For example, in *My Sister Eileen*, Eileen, in her youth, buried a doll on Good Friday to see if it would rise. In *The Yearling*, the grandmother explains at length why she would not want to go to heaven:

"Now I don't want to go to Heaven," she announced.
Ma Baxter said, "Reckon there's no dander."
Grandma's black eyes snapped.
"Why wouldn't you want to go, Grandma?" Jody asked.
"One thing, the company I'd have to keep."
Ma Baxter ignored this.
"Another thing's the music. There's nothin' played there, they claim, but harps. Now the only music I like is a flute and a bass viol and an octave harp. Unless one o' your preachers'll guarantee that, I'll just refuse the trip

with thanks."[42]

These light-hearted comments indicate a trend, but they do not really explain it.

The explanation comes in other forms. It comes in *The Strange Woman* where the two characters who practice religion the most piously are the two most evil characters in the book. It comes in *The Razor's Edge* when Larry Darrell explains that he has never accepted the Christian God because of all the tragic results caused by Christianity:

I couldn't but surmise that the devil, looking at the cruel wars that Christianity has occasioned, the persecutions, the tortures Christian has inflicted on Christian, the unkindness, the hypocrisy, the intolerance, must consider the balance sheet with complacency. And when he remembers that it has laid upon mankind the bitter burden of the sense of sin that has darkened the beauty of the starry night and cast a baleful shadow on the passing pleasures of a world to be enjoyed, he must chuckle as he murmurs: give the devil his due.[43]

The same sort of disillusionment is shown in *The Robe* when Demetrius explains that the last day he prayed was the day that his home was broken up and his family taken for slaves. Because Zeus did not hear their prayers and let the evil fall on them, Demetrius gave up his god. After the causes of disillusionment became known, characters in *The Robe* began inventing their idea of a perfect god. He sounded like a Christian God. The major difference was that he was to practice what he preached. Marcellus and Paulus in *The Robe* invent a god who will eliminate injustice, cure ills and generally fix up the world.

This book holds out the hope that it is the Christian God, but in a discussion in *Escape,* no such hope is extended. The conversation is between Emily Ritter, who is trying to escape from Nazi Germany and Dr. Ditten, the prison doctor who helps her. First she hopes and then he replies:

"If I were God and making a creature like myself I'd give him an eternal life. It would be a conscious life of the spirit with a little of the earthly love and joy I've learned here thrown in. And I'd let him find out about it somehow in advance.

. . . But it's curious that we can bear to live all our lives never really hoping, isn't it? For a long time I've had to live as though that kind of God didn't exist."

"I never think about God."[44]

God has also been given up by the ex-preacher Jim Casy in *The Grapes of Wrath*, but for a different reason. His lust made him feel guilty and evil, then he figured it out. This quotation expresses a theme that is central to this world period. For that reason, it is worth repeating.

> I figgered about the Holy Sperit and the Jesus road. I figgered, 'Why do we got to hang it on God or Jesus? Maybe,' I figgered, 'maybe it's all men an' all women we love; maybe that's the Holy Sperit—the human sperit—the whole she-bang. Maybe all men got one big soul ever'body's a part of.' Now I sat there thinkin' it, an' all of a suddent—I knew it. I knew it so deep down that it was true, and I still know it.[45]

This emphasis on human love as opposed to the spiritual indicates the other important trend. If religion no longer helps define the value system then some substitute must. This substitute is a human morality, consciously a-religious. Jim Casy is one example of this. Another occurs in *So Well Remembered* when the local priest, Father Wendover, tells the reform-minded Mayor Boswell: "I think you're much more like a Christian than many people who come to my Church."[46] His deeds, not his faith, prove his goodness. In the best sellers, everyone acknowledges that morality remains after gods have disappeared. In *For Whom the Bell Tolls*, one of the revolutionaries puts it another way. They are talking about all the shooting and Anselmo says: ". . . with or without God, I think it is a sin to kill."[47] One of his objections to the killing is the brutalizing effect he fears it will have on the killers who themselves survive.

In all of this, what is most important is life—human life, individuals and groups, here on earth. Jim Casy sums it all up in his funeral speech for Grandpa in *The Grapes of Wrath*:

> This here ol' man jus' lived a life an' jus' died out of it. I don't know whether he was good or bad, but that don't matter much. He was alive, an' that's what matters. An' now he's dead, an' that don't matter. Heard a fella tell a poim one time, an' he says, 'All that lives is holy.' Got to thinkin', an' purty soon it means more than the words says. An' I woudln' pray for a ol' fella that's dead. He's awright. He got a job to do, but it's all laid out for 'im an' there's on'y one way to do it. But us, we got a job to do, an' they's a

> thousan' ways, an' we don' know which one to take. An' if I was to pray, it'd be for the folks that don' know which way to turn. Grampa here, he got the easy straight. An' now cover 'im up and let 'im get to his work.[48]

What, one might ask, was new in all this? During the twenties authors asserted the importance of the individual and some rebelled against religion. That is true, but the stylized rebels were only half-men, as were those scared figures of the thirties who were trying to cling to tradition because it was all they had. Now all the parts of man have been brought together and he has been made whole. Finally there has been a recognition that man is in part a religious creature, in part a political, economic, and social creature. And it has been recognized further that all the institutions, separately and together, affect the life of the individual man. He can affect them and they him. It is that realization that resulted in the complexities in the best sellers written in 1938 and afterwards. From here on, man can no longer be viewed as a simple or one-sided being. Too many threats were affecting men's inner lives. Too many people had been too aware of at least one of the forces for too long a time. The simplicity of separating the different parts of man's life could no longer hold up in the obviously complex outside world.

CHAPTER 7

CONCLUSIONS

The novels presented in the past chapters help to reveal changes in the attitudes and values held by the American middle and upper middle classes, especially of the urban North and Far West, during the period of time spanned by World War I and World War II. Several major patterns can be seen. One main trend is the movement of interest from the individual to concern with social and institutional phenomena. There is an increasing awareness that these affect all individuals and therefore are important in and of themselves. Corresponding with this is a changed view of the world as presented in the novels. The early books generally contain a fragmented world in which individuals or small groups of individuals exist without much apparent contact with any but their immediate environment. Gradually, the world becomes interrelated to the point where, in the novels of 1938 to 1945, all the broad social forces and major institutions are shown to be important both in their own right and because they have such a large impact on the lives of individuals. The interaction among these forces, institutions and individual lives is realized. It is primarily in the novels of the last period that political, social, religious, and personal concerns are all combined in the same book.

From 1914 to 1945, the world and life reflected in these novels changed from simple to very complex. The increasing awareness of complexity can be described as growing up or coming of age. This coming of age is accompanied by a decline in absolute values. The more mature writers and readers understand situations in which values are relative, in which there often is no definite right or wrong. This holds true particularly in the area of personal freedoms. During the time from 1914 to 1945, the interest of middle and upper class readers is held by a greater and greater variety of people with an increasingly greater variety of values. Furthermore, the recognition of complexity results in characters who are more fully portrayed individuals than are the stereotyped figures of the earlier novels.

Thus, a framework of the gradual change that took place in the novels that appeared from 1914 to 1945 can be seen. Interest moves from the simple and stereotyped to the complex, from absolutes to relatives, from the isolated individual to social and institutional forces, from a fragmented world to a world in which everything is interrelated. The nature and rate of these changes can be reviewed in a brief survey of several of the major topics studied.

Interest in international affairs and politics develops gradually with the growing recognition of the interrelated nature of the world. During the early period, from 1914 to 1916, international politics are ignored, despite the war, and the only books peopled significantly by foreigners are those written by foreigners. Foreigners generally are ignored. The main characters are Americans living in America. During the period following World War I there is some reaction to the war. There is recognition of soldierly heroism and of the tragedy of war. Also there is some identification with British patriotism. All of these, however, are basically concerns of individuals. The tendency to avoid broader questions of politics and policies appears to express revulsion with them. There is then little interest in international politics expressed in the second group of novels. However an important change does take place during the period 1918 to 1927. This is the internationalization of the characters. Suddenly they form a very cosmopolitan group and, in fact, Europeans appear in some ways superior to Americans.

The novels of the period 1928 to 1937 continue to present an international cast of characters, yet they express an even stronger distrust of world politics. Several books point out specifically that governments hold the responsibility for war and its horrors. There is still no attempt to reform the system, nor is any concern expressed for the totalitarianism rising in the world. The theoretical condemnation does, however, mark a beginning interest. In the mysteries, international politics plays no important role. Only in the books of the last period is there a recognition that the only way to deal with international problems is to get involved with them.

Finally, just before our entry into World War II, the novelists do express concern for what is happening in Europe. There is a gradual recognition that American strength implies American responsibility. As World War II is fought, it is presented as a just cause, worth American involvement. Furthermore, suggestions are made during the course of the war that American responsibility would have to continue after the war. Thus, in the area of international relations, the values expressed in the novels change from isolationism to interest in individuals from other parts of the world to a more general concern for international politics and action. Perhaps the increased cosmopolitanism on a personal level was a prerequisite for the broader commitment.

Developments in attitudes towards domestic politics followed a similar pattern. During the early period, 1914 to 1916, there is a slight expression of the idea that politics are corrupt and in need of reform. During the period 1918 to 1927, there is some criticism of enforced conformity in political thought and some slight suggestion that our system ought to be such that all individuals are given a chance to rise in it. Yet again the characters do not act to bring about reform. The change in attitudes begins in the 1928 to 1937 period. Now a few characters begin to get involved in politics for the sake of achieving particular ends of their own. In addition there is the reassertion of self-reliance in opposition to New Deal collective action. This anti-welfare position is the strongest expression of domestic political values up to this point. The mysteries present a varied view of local politicians. Sometimes they are corrupt, sometimes stupid, sometimes reasonably efficient. Again, the most significant fact is that politics plays some role.

The largest change in attitudes towards domestic political concerns occurs during the period 1938 to 1945. The acceptance of the philosophy of the New Deal takes place during this period. A number of books express the philosophy that the government should be responsible for the well-being of the citizens. The goal is the perfection of the American system, not its destruction. As in the attitudes towards international politics, the novels of the years 1938 to 1945 mark an integration of concern for individuals and recognition of the importance of the institutions of government.

In racial questions there is also a movement from no interest to individual situations and then to a more generalized concern for ethnic problems. However the development of attitudes here does not follow as regular a pattern as it does in changes in political attitudes. In the group of novels published from 1914 to 1916 the leading characters are all whites of Northern European descent. The few representatives of other ethnic groups are stereotypes. Negroes range from poor unfortunates who need to be cared for to savages with strong violent tendencies. Jews tend to be money-loving. Other ethnic groups receive almost no portrayal. In the next group of novels, those appearing from 1918 to 1927, attitudes change significantly. The leading characters remain predominantly Northern Europeans and Americans of Northern European background, but there is a beginning opposition to racial discrimination and stereotyping. A few characters assert that Negroes are individuals with feelings, and one white character actually fights for their political rights. Furthermore, there is a strong effort made to counteract the stereotyped portrayal of Jews. Latin Americans also appear as full human beings, although Southern and Eastern Europeans are neglected. Again, the first step lies in concern for individuals, not a generalized social situation. In the novels published from 1928 to 1927, the stereotypes return in a slightly modified form. Negroes are incapable of caring for themselves and Jews are primarily businessmen who live in a separate social world. Apparently toleration gave way in the atmosphere of fear during the Depression. The mystery stories also tend to uphold the stereotypes.

The most significant change, once again, takes place in the last group of novels. Ethnic discrimination is of central concern in several novels and many more attack it as a social phenomenon. The plight of the individual is viewed in its social context. Generally there is a rejection of stereotyping of Jews, Orientals, and Southern and Eastern Europeans. Negroes receive more varied treatment. Some novelists still portray them as mentally inferior, but other writers assert equality. The evils of race hatred and segregation are shown. Thus, in the area of ethnic problems, once again concern for individuals has developed into more generalized assertions of social concern by the end of the Depression era.

Just as there is development in the presentation and characterization of people of different nationalities and races, there is also a change in the evaluation and role of members of different social and economic classes. The novels of the first period, 1914 to 1916, contain largely middle and upper middle class characters. Members of the lower class are usually depicted as stereotypes who lack individualism, either ignorant servants or poor children who strive to better themselves. The wealthy also appear in two stereotyped forms: those who are improved by their contact with the real world of the middle class and those nouveaux riches who are uncultured and crude. In the novels that appeared from 1918 to 1927, the questioning of the traditional middle class values is accompanied by a decline in the relative importance of middle class characters. A few lower class people are portrayed as having the full range of human emotions. More important is the fact that wealth is no longer condemned and, indeed, is often a prerequisite for adventure, which is judged good. Wealth, realistically, is judged useful. Furthermore, in the pursuit of excitement for the individual, most characters tend to ignore questions of social status. During the period 1928 to 1937 class antagonism again shows itself. The rich sometimes appear as exploiters. The superiority of the middle class and its traditional virtues of hard work and self-reliance is reasserted. Lower class characters continue to play increasingly important roles in the novels. Now there is concern for the personal tragedies caused by poverty but still no interest in social action to improve their lot. The mysteries present few lower class characters. Middle and upper class characters predominate. There is however no general stereotyping. The period 1938 to 1945 again marks the big change to width of view. Members of all classes are fully portrayed individuals. In addition, there is an awareness of the difficulties of poverty, and there is some support for social change and institutional responsibility for economic welfare. This is an important change from the individual charity given by characters in earlier novels.

In the area of more personal considerations, there are corresponding changes in values. As the world view grows broader and gives recognition to complexity, so too the individuals grow more complex, less stereotyped, less forced to conform to certain local standards and more free to choose a variety of differing ways of living and believing. Generally, in the early books, a few patterns predominate. In the more recent books, there is a great variety. Personal freedom grows as the years pass.

The presentation of family life shows a marked development. In the novels of the first group, 1914 to 1916, the family is treated as an almost sacred unit. Relations between children and parents dominate. In fact, in the oversimplified works of the novels of this time, children play a more important role than they do afterwards. Children are portrayed as innocents, to be instructed, and the values of the parents tend to prevail in what usually end up as loving relationships. During the next period, 1918 to 1927, a shift from interest in innocence and purity to interest in experience is accompanied by a change to predominantly older characters and an emphasis on relationships between husbands and wives. There is a recognition that marriages often have problems which are insoluble. There is a decline in family solidarity marked not only by marital disagreements but also by conscious rebellion on the part of adolescent and grown children. Both divorces and affairs take place in these books, often conveying a connotation of daring to break with the old conventions.

In the books published from 1928 to 1937 there is on this point a continuation, rather than a break, in development. Relationships between adult members of families predominate. Furthermore, family friction is now accepted as normal and is no longer largely the product of a conscious rebellion by the children or by women seeking independence. There is a realistic variety in family relations. Disharmony is presented as having individual causes, not as a product of a generation gap or a generalized rebellion. Generally the mystery stories follow the pattern of the novels of 1928 to 1937. The books of the last period, 1938 to 1945, recognize a variety of family relationships and treat both those between children and parents and those between husbands and wives. But now the reasons for both harmony and enmity are explored. There is not a rebelliousness for its own sake on the part of the younger generation, but often children break with their parents over specific issues. They are the products of the new social consciousness. Divorces and affairs are commonplace, but again there is now an exploration of the causes.

The depiction of sex changes in a steady pattern. The books of the first group contain almost no descriptions of sexual acts, nor are acts beyond exciting first kisses implied. The authors of the best sellers that appeared between 1918 and 1927 write only a little more descriptive narrative of physical acts, but they do convey the idea that such acts take place. In the books that were published from 1928 to 1937, there is a considerable amount of description of sexual activities and one discussion of how to get an abortion. The mysteries, like the novels of the post-World War I period, contain no such descriptions although they make it clear that people do participate. The novels published from 1938 to 1945 do not initiate any great change in this area. They simply carry further the tendency towards increased vividness of description of sexual activities and increased individual choice in personal behavior. From these examples it can be seen that in the area of the very personal activities and values relating to family life and sex life, the change takes place in a steady pattern. No relapse or retrogression occurs in the novels of the period 1928 to 1937 as it does in attitudes that relate to society as a whole.

The views on the position of women, as related to that of men, follows a pattern in these novels similar to those on social questions. In the books that appeared from 1914 to 1916, male characters are central in the stories and they dominate female characters. Women generally are portrayed as pure creatures who are to be honored. Their lives are limited to their homes, except for a few single women who hold a limited number of jobs until they find husbands. During the period of conscious rebellion, 1918 to 1927, men are no longer either as central to the stories or as dominant over women. Women also follow a wider variety of professions and exotic hobbies. The novels published from 1928 to 1937 mark a partial retrogression in that men again are more central to the stories and more dominant over women. Women do, however, continue to hold a wide variety of jobs. The same situation is true in the mysteries. By the time of the appearance of the last group of novels, 1938 to 1945, the strong role of women is restored. The rebellions of the twenties are now accepted. Those women who are dominated by men have chosen to be so. The definition of the comparative roles of the sexes then follows the patterns of social change rather than those of development of personal values.

Religious belief, as presented in the best sellers, follows a totally different pattern of change than do either social attitudes or personal values. Interest in religion is strongest in the novels that appeared between 1914 and 1916. No rebellion against formal religion takes place except in the books by British authors. The way in which religion is most important, however, is in the application of religious principles to everyday life, not in terms of abstract theory or belief. The low point of interest in religion appears in the novels written from 1918 to 1927. A conscious acceptance of a variety of beliefs takes place. It is asserted that no one formal morality should be considered superior to another. Christianity is criticized both for its hypocrisy and because of the existence of dishonest ministers. Formal Christianity also receives some condemnation for its emphasis on an afterlife rather than on the world here and now. The period of retreat from new social ideas, 1928 to 1937, also marks a return to spiritual belief and concern. Generally the interest lies in a spiritual basis of man's treatment of man. In the mysteries religion holds no particular importance, but it is not rebelled against. It is just ignored. The most profound differences of opinion on religion are expressed in the novels that appeared from 1938 to 1945. Some books refute religion and express a disillusionment with a God that could allow evil. Other books recognize the religious impulse and express an understanding of people who seek the support of firm belief. Throughout, however, there is more interest in earth than in heaven. Deeds, not belief, must prove goodness. The new and conscious assertion is that morality remains even if the gods have disappeared.

The new morality is the change in attitudes towards social questions and the change in personal values that has been seen in this study of best selling novels. The new morality does not require the existence of gods. It centers around human life. It asserts that all people have both certain freedoms and certain rights. They are free to determine their own religious and philosophical beliefs and they are free to follow their own sexual morality. Furthermore, all men, regardless of race or class, have the right to an opportunity for a good life. After all men are recognized as individuals who desire this, then caring for individuals develops into a broader responsibility. Assurance of individual rights, in the admittedly complex world, has become a matter of social and institutional concern and responsibility. It is this recognition, that is reflected largely in the novels of 1938 to 1945, that reflects the emergence of a mature American middle and upper class willing to cope with the complexities of the modern world.

APPENDIX A

AMERICAN BEST-SELLING FICTION, 1914-1945

The following is a list of the novels used in this study. They are listed chronologically, according to their listing in Frank Luther Mott, *Golden Multitudes* (New York, 1947), pp. 313-315, 325-329. This is Mott's total list. His list of top best sellers is indicated by a + before the book. A top best seller is defined as any book which, during its total life, has sold a number of copies equal to one per cent of the population of the United States at the beginning of the decade in which it was first issued. It should be noted that the largest sale usually took place within the first few years after publication. The rest of the books listed are those which Mott describes as coming close to the required total sale.

The books in this list which also made the top ten listing for any one year are indicated with a *. These ratings are calculated only from the sale of the editions issued by the original publisher and do not include reprint editions or book club sales. The annual lists are compiled in Alice Payne Hackett, *Sixty Years of Best Sellers* 1895-1955 (New York, 1956), pp. 119-183.

Books are listed chronologically and within each year in alphabetical order according to the author's last name. The rest of the information given identifies the particular edition of each novel which was used in making this study.

+	1914	Burroughs, Edgar Rice. *Tarzan of the Apes.* Racine: Whitman Publishing Company, 1964.
+ *	1914	Tarkington, Booth. *Penrod.* New York: Doubleday, Page and Company, 1914.
+ *	1914	Wright, Harold Bell. *The Eyes of the World.* Chicago: Book Supply Company, 1914.
	1915	Maugham, Somerset. *Of Human Bondage.* Garden City: Doubleday, Doran and Company, 1915.
*	1915	Porter, Eleanor H. *Pollyanna Grows Up.* Boston: The Page Company, 1915.
+ *	1915	Porter, Gene Stratton. *Michael O'Halloran.* New York: Grosset and Dunlap, n.d.
	1915	Rinehart, Mary Roberts. "*K.*" Boston: Houghton, Mifflin Company, 1915.

* 1915 Tarkington, Booth. *The Turmoil.* New York: Harper Brothers, 1915.

* 1916 Porter, Eleanor H. *Just David.* Boston: Houghton, Mifflin Company, 1916.

* 1916 Tarkington, Booth. *Seventeen.* Garden City: Doubleday, Page and Company, 1916.

* 1916 Wells, H. G. *Mr. Britling Sees It Through.* New York: MacMillan Company, 1916.

+ * 1916 Wright, Harold Bell. *When a Man's a Man.* New York: A. L. Burt Company, 1916.

* 1918 Blasco Ibanez, Vincente. *The Four Horsemen of the Apocalypse.* New York: E. P. Dutton and Company, 1919.

* 1918 Streeter, Edward. *Dere Mable.* New York, Frederick A. Stokes Co., 1918.

* 1919 Wright, Harold Bell. *The Re-Creation of Brian Kent.* Chicago: The Book Supply Company, 1919.

* 1920 Grey, Zane. *The Man of the Forest.* New York: Grosset and Dunlap, n.d.

* 1920 Lewis, Sinclair. *Main Street.* New York: Signet Classics, 1963.

+ * 1920 Oppenheim, E. Phillips. *The Great Impersonation.* Boston: Little, Brown and Company, 1920.

* 1921 Canfield, Dorothy. *The Brimming Cup.* New York: Harcourt, Brace and Company, 1921.

* 1921 Grey, Zane. *The Mysterious Rider.* New York: Harper and Brothers, 1921.

+ * 1921 Hull, Edith M. *The Sheik.* Boston: Small, Maynard and Company, 1921.

* 1921 Hutchinson, A. S. M. *If Winter Comes.* New York: Grosset and Dunlap, 1921.

1921 Sabatini, Rafael. *Scaramouche.* Boston: Houghton, Mifflin Company, 1921.

* 1921 Wharton, Edith. *The Age of Innocence.* New York: Grosset and Dunlap, 1921.

1922 Hough, Emerson. *The Covered Wagon.* New York: D. Appleton Company, 1926.

* 1922 Lewis, Sinclair. *Babbitt.* New York: Signet Books, 1961.

* 1923 Atherton, Gertrude. *Black Oxen.* New York: Boni and Liveright, 1923.

* 1923 Sabatini, Rafael. *The Sea Hawk.* New York: Popular Library, 1961.

* 1924 Ferber, Edna. *So Big.* New York: Doubleday, Doran and Company, 1924.

1924 Milne, A. A. *When We Were Very Young.* New York: E. P. Dutton and Company, 1924.

* 1924 Sedgwick, Anne Douglas. *The Little French Girl.* Boston: Houghton, Mifflin Company, 1924.

+ 1924 Wodehouse, P. G. *Jeeves.* New York: George H. Doran Company, 1924.

* 1925 Erskine, John. *The Private Life of Helen of Troy.* New York: Grosset and Dunlap, 1925.

* 1925 Kennedy, Margaret. *The Constant Nymph.* Garden City: Doubleday, Page and Company, 1925.

* 1925 Loos, Anita. *Gentlemen Prefer Blondes.* New York: Boni and Liveright, 1925.

* 1925 Wren, Christopher. *Beau Geste.* Philadelphia: J. B. Lippincott Company, 1925.

1926 Biggers, Earl Derr. *The Chinese Parrot.* New York: Paperback Library, 1963.

1926 Christie, Agatha. *The Murder of Roger Ackroyd.* New York: Pocket Books, 1926.

* 1926 Deeping, Warwick. *Sorrell and Son.* New York: Grosset and Dunlap, 1926.

+ 1926 Smith, Thorne. *Topper.* New York: Pocket Books, 1941.

1927 Hart, Frances Noyes. *The Bellamy Trial.* Garden City: Doubleday and Company, 1927.

* 1927 Lewis, Sinclair. *Elmer Gantry.* New York: Harcourt, Brace and Company, 1927.

* 1927 Wilder, Thornton. *The Bridge of San Luis Rey.* New York: Albert and Charles Boni, 1927.

1927 Van Dine, S. S. *The Canary Murder Case.* New York: Pocket Books, 1943.

1928 Biggers, Earl Derr. *Behind That Curtain.* Indianapolis: Bobbs-Merrill Company, 1928.

* 1928 Delmar, Vina. *Bad Girl.* New York: Harcourt, Brace

and Company, 1928.

+ * 1929 Douglas, Lloyd C. *The Magnificent Obsession.* New York: Grosset and Dunlap, n.d.

1929 Hammett, Dashiell. *Red Harvest.* In *The Novels of Dashiell Hammett.* New York: Alfred A. Knopf, 1965.

* 1929 Remarque, Erich Maria. *All Quiet on the Western Front.* New York: Fawcett World Library, 1961.

* 1929 Van Dine, S. S. *The Bishop Murder Case.* New York: Charles Scribner's Sons, 1929.

1930 Bentley, E. C. *Trent's Last Case.* New York: Alfred A. Knopf, 1930.

1930 Biggers, Earl Derr. *Charlie Chan Carries On.* New York: Paperback Library, 1964.

1930 Brand, Max. *Destry Rides Again.* In *Max Brand's Fiction Rodeo.* New York: Grosset and Dunlap, 1931.

* 1930 Ferber, Edna. *Cimarron.* New York: Grosset and Dunlap, 1930.

1930 Hammett, Dashiell. *The Maltese Falcon.* In *The Novels of Dashiell Hammett.* New York: Alfred A. Knopf, 1965.

1930 Queen, Ellery. *The French Powder Mystery.* New York: Frederick A. Stokes, 1930.

+ * 1931 Buck, Pearl. *The Good Earth.* New York: Pocket Books, 1964.

1931 Charteris, Leslie. *Enter the Saint.* New York: Fiction Publishing Company, n.d.

1931 Hammett, Dashiell. *The Glass Key.* New York: Alfred A. Knopf, 1931.

+ 1931 Queen, Ellery. *The Dutch Shoe Mystery.* New York: F. A. Stokes Company, 1931.

1932 Christie, Agatha. *Peril at End House.* New York: Pocket Books, 1965.

+ 1932 Queen, Ellery. *The Egyptian Cross Mystery.* New York: F. A. Stokes Company, 1932.

+ * 1933 Allen, Hervey. *Anthony Adverse.* New York: Farrar and Rhinehart, Inc., 1933.

1933 Caldwell, Erskine. *God's Little Acre.* New York:

Signet Books, 1949.

+ 1933 Gardner, Erle Stanley. *The Case of the Sulky Girl.* London: George Harrap and Company, 1934.

1933 Gardner, Erle Stanley. *The Case of the Velvet Claws.* New York: Pocket Books, 1963.

1933 Gardner, Erle Stanley. *The Case of the Lucky Legs.* New York: Walter J. Black, 1934.

+ * 1933 Hilton, James. *Lost Horizon.* New York: Pocket Books, 1966.

+ 1934 Gardner, Erle Stanley. *The Case of the Curious Bride.* New York: Pocket Books, 1956.

* 1934 Hilton, James. *Goodbye, Mr. Chips.* Boston: Little, Brown and Company, 1934.

1934 Queen, Ellery. *The Adventures of Ellery Queen.* New York: Pocket Books, 1947.

+ 1934 Queen, Ellery. *The Chinese Orange Mystery.* New York: International Readers League, 1934.

* 1935 Douglas, Lloyd C. *Green Light.* Boston: Houghton, Mifflin Company, 1935.

1935 Gardner, Erle Stanley. *The Case of the Caretaker's Cat.* New York: Pocket Books, 1963.

+ 1935 Gardner, Erle Stanley. *The Case of the Counterfeit Eye.* New York: Pocket Books, 1965.

1935 Queen, Ellery. *The Spanish Cape Mystery.* New York: Pocket Books, 1962.

* 1936 Edmonds, W. D. *Drums Along the Mohawk.* Boston: Little, Brown and Company, 1936.

+ 1936 Gardner, Erle Stanley. *The Case of the Stuttering Bishop.* New York: Pocket Books, 1966.

1936 Latimer, Jonathan. *Lady in the Morgue.* New York: The Sun Dial Press, 1937.

+ * 1936 Mitchell, Margaret. *Gone With the Wind.* New York: Pocket Books, 1965.

1936 Stout, Rex. *The Rubber Band.* New York: Pocket Books, 1945.

* 1937 Cronin, A. J. *The Citadel.* New York: Bantam Books, 1962.

+ 1937 Gardner, Erle Stanley. *The Case of the Dangerous Dowager.* New York: Pocket Books, 1953.

\+ 1937 Gardner, Erle Stanley. *The Case of the Lame Canary.* New York: Pocket Books, 1966.

* 1937 Roberts, Kenneth. *Northwest Passage.* Garden City: Doubleday, Doran and Company, 1936.

\+ 1938 Brand, Max. *Singing Guns.* New York. Dodd, Mead and Company, 1938.

* 1938 duMaurier, Daphne. *Rebecca.* New York: Doubleday, Doran and Company, 1938.

* 1938 Field, Rachel. *All This, and Heaven Too.* New York: Dell Paperback, 1963.

\+ 1938 Gardner, Erle Stanley. *The Case of the Substitute Face.* New York: Pocket Books, 1953.

1938 McKenney, Ruth. *My Sister Eileen.* New York: Harcourt, Brace and Company, 1938.

\+ 1938 Page, Marco. *Fast Company.* New York: Dodd, Mead and Company, 1938.

* 1938 Rawlings, Marjorie Kinnan. *The Yearling.* New York: Charles Scribner's Sons, 1938.

\+ 1938 Runyon, Damon. *The Best of Damon Runyon.* Philadelphia: Blakiston Company, 1945.

1939 Ambler, Eric. *Coffin for Dimitrios.* In *Intrigue.* New York: Alfred A. Knopf, 1960.

* 1939 Asch, Sholem. *The Nazarene.* New York: G. P. Putnam's Sons, 1939.

1939 Charteris, Leslie. *The Happy Highwayman.* New York: Doubleday, Doran and Company, 1939.

1939 Christie, Agatha. *Easy to Kill.* New York: Pocket Books, 1965.

* 1939 Morley, Christopher. *Kitty Foyle.* Philadelphia: J.B. Lippincott Company, 1939.

+* 1939 Steinbeck, John. *The Grapes of Wrath.* New York: Bantam Books, 1955.

* 1939 Vance, Ethel. *Escape.* Boston: Little, Brown and Company, 1939.

1940 Ambler, Eric. *Journey Into Fear.* New York: Alfred A. Knopf, 1940.

1940 Chandler, Raymond. *Farewell My Lovely.* New York: Pocket Books, 1964.

1940 Christie, Agatha. *And Then There Were None.* New

York: Pocket Books, 1964.

* 1940 Hemingway, Ernest. *For Whom the Bell Tolls.* New York: Charles Scribner's Sons, 1940.

1940 Knight, Eric. *Lassie-Come-Home.* Chicago: John C. Winston Company, 1940.

* 1940 Llewellyn, Richard. *How Green Was My Valley.* New York: MacMillan Company, 1956.

+ 1940 Queen, Ellery. *New Adventures of Ellery Queen.* New York: Triangle Books, 1943.

* 1940 Roberts, Kenneth. *Oliver Wiswell.* New York: Doubleday, Doran and Company, 1940.

+* 1940 Struther, Jan. *Mrs. Miniver.* New York: Harcourt, Brace and Company, 1942.

1941 Christie, Agatha. *The Patriotic Murders.* New York: Dodd, Mead and Company, 1941.

* 1941 Cronin, A. J. *The Keys of the Kingdom.* Boston: Little, Brown and Company, 1941.

+* 1941 Hilton, James. *Random Harvest.* Boston: Little, Brown and Company, 1941.

1941 MacInnes, Helen. *Above Suspicion.* New York: Harcourt, Brace and Company, 1941.

* 1941 Miller, Alice Duer. *The White Cliffs of Dover.* New York: Coward-McCann, Inc., 1941.

1941 O'Hara, Mary. *My Friend Flicka.* Philadelphia: J. B. Lippincott Company, 1941.

1941 Williams, Ben Ames. *Strange Woman.* Cambridge: Houghton, Mifflin Company, 1941.

* 1942 Buck, Pearl S. *Dragon Seed.* New York: John Day Company, 1942.

* 1942 Davenport, Marcia. *The Valley of Decision.* New York: Charles Scribner's Sons, 1942.

+* 1942 Douglas, Lloyd C. *The Robe.* Boston: Houghton, Mifflin Company, 1947.

1942 Runyon, Damon. *Damon Runyon Favorites.* New York: Pocket Books, 1942.

* 1942 Steen, Marguerite. *The Sun is My Undoing.* New York: The Viking Press, 1942.

* 1942 Steinbeck, John. *The Moon is Down.* New York: Viking Press, 1942.

* 1942 Werfel, Franz. *The Song of Bernadette.* New York: The Viking Press, 1942.

* 1943 Asch, Sholem. *The Apostle.* New York: G. P. Putnam's Sons, 1943.

1943 Franken, Rose. *Claudia.* New York: Pocket Books, 1945.

* 1943 Marquand, John P. *So Little Time.* Boston: Little, Brown and Company, 1943.

1943 Marshall, Rosamond. *Kitty.* New York: Pocket Books, 1948.

* 1943 Saroyan, William. *The Human Comedy.* New York: Overseas Editions, Inc., 1943.

+ * 1943 Smith, Betty. *A Tree Grows in Brooklyn.* Philadelphia: The Blakiston Company, n.d.

* 1944 Cronin, A. J. *The Green Years.* Boston: Little, Brown and Company, 1944.

+ * 1944 Goudge, Elizabeth. *Green Dolphin Street.* New York: Coward-McCann Company, 1944.

+ * 1944 Graham, Gwethalyn. *Earth and High Heaven.* Philadelphia: J. B. Lippincott Company, 1944.

* 1944 Hersey, John. *A Bell for Adano.* New York: Alfred A Knopf, 1944.

+ * 1944 Maugham, Somerset. *The Razor's Edge.* Garden City: Doubleday, Doran and Company, 1944.

1944 Seton, Anya. *Dragonwyck.* Boston: Houghton, Mifflin Company, 1944.

\+ 1944 Sharp, Margery. *Cluny Brown.* Boston: Little, Brown and Company, 1944.

* 1944 Smith, Lillian. *Strange Fruit.* New York: Reynal and Hitchcock, 1944.

* 1944 Williams, Ben Ames. *Leave Her to Heaven.* New York: Bantam Books, 1950.

+ * 1945 Costain, Thomas B. *The Black Rose.* New York: Doubleday, Doran and Company, 1945.

* 1945 Hilton, James. *So Well Remembered.* New York: Pocket Books, 1964.

* 1945 Langley, Adria Locke. *A Lion Is In the Streets.* New York: McGraw Hill Book Company, 1945.

* 1945 Lewis, Sinclair. *Cass Timberlane.* New York: Ran-

com House, 1945.

+ * 1945 Shellabarger, Samuel. *Captain From Castile.* Boston: Little, Brown and Company, 1945.

* 1945 Ullman, James Ramsey. *The White Tower.* Philadelphia: J. B. Lippincott Company, 1945.

+ * 1945 Winsor, Kathleen. *Forever Amber.* New York: Signet Books, 1963.

APPENDIX B

ITEMS FOR RATING EACH NOVEL

Although the novels were studied in a number of different ways, one very helpful tool was the following list of items for which each novel was rated on a 5 to 0 scale. This rating provided a concise overview of the comparative importance of various topics in the novels and also of major changes in values during the period of time studied.

The numbers meant different things for different items, and the definition is given with each item. One of the most common ratings was for importance. To illustrate, in each novel the importance of such elements as humor, race, religion, politics, economic class, education, art, and nature was rated. The scale for importance remains constant. It is as follows:

5 = central concern of the book
4 = major, but not necessarily the only central concern
3 = contributing.factor
2 = minor
1 = only a few indications of views given
0 = no concern

This rating system then allows two kinds of comparisons. It makes clear which concerns are of most importance in a given time period. Furthermore it allows the importance of a given topic to be traced through all the time periods, making changes or continuity observable.

Another common scale rated the author's apparent judgment in a number of areas. A judgment that something was very good gave it a 5; a judgment that it was very evil or corrupt resulted in a 1. For example, formal education might be presented as good and necessary for success. If so, it received a 5. If, on the other hand, education was shown to be corrupting of natural virtue, the item was rated 1. Judgments in the middle received numbers in the middle. Again, this allows for easy comparisons within a time period and among the different time periods.

This system of numerical rating was, in fact, used to determine the time periods in this study. All the ratings were punched into computer cards. A scale of similarity was used to divide the books into those groups in which the books were most similar to each other. The computer did the mathematical operations. The process was done once for all the items and once for selected particularly important items. Both yielded the result that the greatest degrees of similarity fell within the time periods. Those periods thus seemed to be the best framework in which to present the novels. This was the only use made of a computer.

For the most part, these numerical ratings were one tool used to bring together the information on all the novels. The details were always referred to before any definitive statements about content or values were made. A few of the items require verbal rather than numerical information. Including this in the tables of numbers again provided the advantage of having all the information together.

The following is a list of the items and ratings used.

1. Number of book (assigned for identification)
2. Year (as it appears in Frank Mott, *The Golden Multitudes*)
3. Title
4. a. Author's name
   b. Year of birth
   c. Place of birth
   d. Code for area of birth: 1) Northeast U.S. 2) Southeast U.S. 3) Mid-West U.S. 4) West U.S. 5) Foreign
5. Number of pages: 1) 1-100 2) 101-300 3) 301-400 4) 401-500 5) 501 and over
6. a. Time of action: 1) contemporary 2) earlier 20th century

or 19th leading into 20th 3) 19th century 4) 15-18th century 5) earlier

b. Specify if 4 or 5 or it is necessary

c. Purposes: 1) realism 2) social comment 3) analogy to present 4) escape 5) other

d. Specify if 5 or necessary

7. a. Setting (in space put code number for region of U.S. as in 4d)

   b. Type of location: 1) undeveloped non-urban 2) farm, ranch, country estate 3) town 4) small city 5) large city

   c. Purpose: 1) realism 2) exotic–nature good 3) exotic–fantasy 4) idealized 5) other and specify

8. Mystery or not: 5) mystery 0) non-mystery as type of book

9. Style and vocabulary–check in the spaces applicable

   a. sophisticated
   b. straightforward or easy
   c. colloquial
   d. use of profanity or vulgarisms (God damn or more serious)
   e. use of technical terms–specify field
   f. use of foreign words or phrases
   g. regional dialect
   h. class dialect
   i. obvious preaching–didacticism
   j. other–specify

10. Humor

   a. Use of: 5) most important 4) a lot but not central 3) moderate 2) a little 1) rare 0) none
   b. Importance of family humor, within the general category of humor: 5-0 as above
   c. Importance of ethnic humor–as above
   d. Humor in day-to-day interaction–as above
   e. Humor in attack on accepted values or authorities–as above
   f. Humor at an individual's expense–as above
   g. Humor as satire–as above
   h. other–specify

   Note: General scale for rating importance, when no other

categorization is specified: 5) central 4) major 3) contributing factor 2) minor 1) a few indications 0) no consideration of the topic
(0) always means no consideration of any given topic unless otherwise specified

11. Race
    a. Importance
    b. 5) Characters mainly WASPs and no discussion of racial issues 4) Characters mainly WASPs and only a little discussion of racial issues 0) Characters not mainly WASPs
    c. White Northern Europeans: 5) Physically and mentally superior 4) morally and mentally superior 3) physically superior 2) just people 1) inferior
    d. Jews: 5) superior 4) just people 3) scholarly, intellectual, but physically inferior or generally nice but separated out from others by racial characteristics 2) tricky, defensive, greedy 1) villains–really evil
    e. Negroes: 5) admired 4) just people 3) to be cared for–nice 2) slaves, servants, or particularly ignorant 1) animals–criminals
    f. Orientals: 5) admired 4) just people 3) slightly stupid or odd 2) servants 1) criminal, sneaky
    g. Southern and Eastern Europeans: 5) admired 4) just people 3) untrained, uneducated lower class 2) stupid, lazy, dirty 1) criminal
    h. Highest intolerance–d, e, f, g, and other

12. Religion
    a. Importance
    b. General rightness: 1) dogma and institution, specific references to God as accepted by organized religion 2) morality 3) lip service 2) nothing 1) criticism or making fun of institutionalized religion or belief
    c. Rightness of Catholicism–as above
    d. Rightness of Protestantism–as above
    e. Rightness of Judaism–as above
    f. Rightness of Oriental religions, including Islam–as above
    g. Rightness of Agnosticism–as above
    h. Rightness of Atheism–as above

i. Toleration of other religions: 5) fight for toleration 4) toleration accepted 3) no issue 2) conversational criticism 1) persecution

13. Nature of man
    a. 5) good 4) mild good 3) can be anything 2)mild evil 1) evil
    b. Changes in character: 5) complete reversals 4) improvement only 3) circumstances primary 2) minor changes 1) no changes
    c. Judgment of people's morality: 5) strong 4) moderate 3) mild, with sympathy 2) none made 1) assertion that none should be made
    d. Good guys vs. bad guys: 5) good always win 4) good lose temporarily then win 3) bad become good and win 2) come out equal 1) no judgment
    e. Determinism: 5) original sin 4) no freedom–born good or bad 3) combination of freedom and determinism 2) values taught early 1) total freedom

14. Politics
    a. International: Importance
    b. International: 5) heroes, strong partisanship 4) vague partisanship 3) no judgment 2) mild criticism, mild reform necessary 1) evil, strong reform necessary
    c. International: 5) strong good and bad 4) moderate 3) no judgment 2) all the work of publicity men 1) people good but politicians evil
    d. Isolationism: 5) involvement 4) involvement with provisions 3) no judgment 2) isolation with provisions 1) strong isolationism
    e. National: Importance
    f. National: as in b
    g. Local: Importance
    h. Local: as in b
    i. Highest importance for all kinds of politics–the highest of a, e, or g

15. Classes of characters
    a. Importance
    b. Importance of upper class characters

c. Importance of middle class characters
d. Importance of lower class characters
e. Importance of upward mobility
f. Importance of downward mobility

16. Class relations
    a. Importance
    b. Attitude of upper class to the middle class—consider them: 5) equal 4) a few individuals equal 3) should be helped or looked up to 2) disdain or leave alone 1) active antagonism
    c. Attitude of upper to lower—as above
    d. Attitude of middle to upper—as above
    e. Attitude of middle to lower—as above
    f. Attitude of lower to upper—as above
    g. Attitude of lower to middle—as above
    h. Average b-g, gives scale for antagonism not corresponding to word definitions
    i. No antagonism—all one class—upper
    j. No antagonism—all one class—middle
    k. No antagonism—all one class—lower

17. List occupations of good or key characters

18. List occupations judged particularly bad

19. Importance of business or occupation

20. Importance of success at occupation for at least one good character

21. Importance of work

22. Importance of skill

23. a. Importance of education
    b. Good of education: 5) good and necessary 4) good 3) neutral 2) not needed 1) corrupting

24. a. Importance of art
    b. Good of art—as 23b
    c. Type of art involved—specify

25. a. Importance of nature
    b. Importance of conflict between nature and civilization
    c. Good of nature: 5) all good—saves people 4) good in

place 3) neutral 2) without comforts 1) threatening

26. Attitudes towards authority by characters judged good: 5) active rebellion 4) not respected 3) partial acceptance, individual judgment put first 2) vague acceptance or acceptance with regret 1) fully accepted at end
    a. Governmental
    b. Religious
    c. Parental
    d. Inner conscience
    e. Job superior
    f. Class superior
    g. Men (over women)
    h. Age (over youth)
    i. Own class custom, social mores, peer group custom
    j. Other
    k. Average
27. Conflicts—first column rated for importance, second column for solution: 5) complete solution, individual and general 4) individual level solved 3) partial solution 2) solution not found 1) no solution shown to exist
    a. Love
    b. Money
    c. Social position
    d. Business superiority
    e. Political authority or power
    f. Personal authority
    g. Beliefs, morality
    h. Class custom vs. conformity of the individual
    i. Racial
    j. Family feud—two or more families or branches of one family
    k. Individual vs. the order of the universe, fate, God, etc.
    l. Mystery—to be solved
    m. Class reform
    n. International
    o. How to run one's family

p. Other
q. Average of conflicts
r. Average of solutions

28. Expectation level and fulfillment of desires. Fill in the appropriate levels only. If no judgment of characters, use good guys spaces. 5) all fulfilled 4) a few compromises 3) compromise 2) lose more than win 1) lose
   a. Good guys: high
   b. Good guys: medium
   c. Good guys: low
   d. Bad guys: high
   e. Bad guys: medium
   f. Bad guys: low

29. Importance of social theme) Must be the same number
30. Importance of individual theme) if of equal importance

31. a. Importance of plot–action
   b. Importance of what happens to the characters–events
   c. Importance of character development–change

32. a. Importance of the story
   b. Importance of commentary on politics
   c. Importance of commentary on morality
   d. Importance of commentary on class and comments on economic matters
   e. Importance of commentary on how to lead one's personal life
   f. Other–specify

33. Units of reference of characters–rate for importance
   a. Individual
   b. Family (to parents and siblings-in-law)
   c. Extended family
   d. School
   e. Business
   f. Small community
   g. City
   h. State

i. Country
j. World
k. Mankind
l. Peer group
m. Friends
n. Other

34. Family relations: 5) very good 4) moderately good 3) neutral–no passion 2) mildly bad–cold 1) active fighting–hate
    a. Children–parents (throughout)
    b. Children–parents (at end)
    c. Husband-wife (throughout)
    d. Husband-wife (at end)
    e. Fidelity: 5) faithful 4) brief lapse and return 3) infidelity and punishment 2) continuing infidelity 1) rupture
    f. Judgment of infidelity: 5) good 4) OK 3) no judgment 2) mildly bad 1) evil
    g. Extended family (throughout)–as above
    h. Extended family (at end)

35. Sex
    a. Marital: 5) very good 4) natural, mildly good 3) neutral 2) cold 1) bad
    b. Description: 5) vivid 4) above waist 3) kissing 2) acknowledgement of physical event or effect but no description 1) mild acknowledgement
    c. Pre-marital–as in a
    d. Description–as in b
    e. Extra-marital–as in a
    f. Description–as in b
    g. Double-standard–men allowed more than women: 5) yes 3) women only if men do 1) equal
    h. Homosexuality: 5) good 4) accepted 3) difficulties emphasized 2) wrong 1) fought
    i. Other

36. Men-women as central: 5) men 4) men a bit 3) equal 2) women a bit 1) women

37. Men-women as dominant: 5) men 4) men–mild dominance 3) equal 2) women–mild dominance 1) women

38. Women as different from men: 5) pure, to be honored, weak, not to work 4) pure, to be honored, only in the home, but strong 3) can work, but should be different 2) equal 1) women masculine

39. Predominant age of characters—rate 5-1 for importance of characters in each group
    a. Old
    b. Mature adults
    c. Young married
    d. Young pre-married
    e. Children
    f. Story goes for more than one generation: 5) yes 0) no

40. Tension: youth vs. age—importance

41. Measure of youth-age domination: 5) youth always 4) youth dominate except when infants—mild 3) equal 2) elders dominate until feeble—mild 1) elders dominate

42. Age distinctions
    a. Importance
    b. Experience leads to 5) understanding and contentment 3) neutral 1) hurtful, dying
    c. Experience leads to 5) greater morality 3) equal 1) moral decay with age
    d. Emphasis on physical decay 5) strong 4) mild 3) equal 2) no mention 1) improvement

43. a. Importance of youth distinction
    b. To be envied
    c. Innocence
    d. To be instructed
    e. Change from youth to age
    f. Different standards of morality
    g. Children a nuisance
    h. Youth as torture to itself
    i. Physically stronger
    j. Other

44. Importance of physical strength

45. View of the military: 5) very good 4) necessary and good 3) necessary and neutral 2) necessary and bad 1) bad

NOTES

CHAPTER 1

[1]James D. Hart, *The Popular Book: A History of America's Literary Taste* (New York, 1950), p. 285. This is a survey of popular books in America from colonial times to 1950.

[2]Robert Banker, "What Makes a Book Sell?", *Publishers' Weekly,* Dec. 4, 1954, Vol. 166, No. 23, pp. 2179-2180. He was assistant manager of the Doubleday Book Shops.

[3]Complete list of Literary Guild selections provided by Margaretha Murphy of the Literary Guild. Letter to the author, April 3, 1969.

[4]*The First 40 Years of the Book-of-the-Month Club,* supplement to *The Book-of-the-Month Club News,* April, 1966, provided by the Book-of-the-Month Club, New York.

[5]*Interesting Facts About the Book-of-the-Month Club and Its Role in American Literary History,* publication of the Book-of-the-Month Club (New York, 1967), p. 5.

[6]*Ibid.,* p. 3.

[7]Frederick Lewis Allen, "Best-Sellers: 1900-1935," *Saturday Review of Literature,* pp. 3-4, 20-26, Dec. 7, 1935, Vol. XIII, No. 6, p. 3.

[8]Philadelphia, 1938.

[9]Bernard Berelson, "Who Reads What Books and Why?", *Saturday Review of Literature,* May 12, 1951, pp. 7-8, 30-31. Reprinted in B. Rosenberg and D. White, eds. *Mass Culture: The Popular Arts in America.*

[10]*Ibid.,* p. 121

[11]*Historical Statistics of the United States,* U.S. Bureau of the Census, Washington, D.C., 1960, p. 214.

[12]*Ibid.,* p. 207.

[13]Irving Harlow Hart, "The One Hundred Leading Authors of Best Sellers in Fiction From 1895 to 1944," *Publishers' Weekly,* Jan. 19, 1946, Vol. 149, No. 3, p. 285.

[14]Douglas Waples, *Research Memorandum on Social Aspects of Reading in the Depression,* Social Science Research Council, Bulletin No. 37, New York, 1937, pp. 129-130, found that women made up slightly more than 50% of the public library readers at the time and place he did his research.

[15]Alan Dutscher, "The Book Business in America," *Contemporary Issues,* April-May, 1954, Vol. 5, pp. 38-58. Reprinted in Rosenberg and White, *op. cit.* All statistics from p. 127.

[16]Louis R. Wilson, *The Geography of Reading* (Chicago, 1938).

[17]*Ibid.,* p. 247.

[18]The regions for Wilson's study are defined as follows: *Far West*: California, Nevada, Oregon, Washington; *North East*: Connecticut, Delaware,

Maine, Maryland, Massachusetts, New Hampshire, New Jersey, New York, Pennsylvania, Rhode Island, Vermont, West Virginia; *Middle West*: Illinois, Indiana, Iowa, Michigan, Minnesota, Missouri, Ohio, Wisconsin; *North West*: Colorado, Idaho, Kansas, Montana, Nebraska, North Dakota, South Dakota, Utah, Wyoming; *South West*: Arizona, New Mexico, Oklahoma, Texas; *South East*: Alabama, Arkansas, Florida, Georgia, Kentucky, Louisiana, Mississippi, North Carolina, South Carolina, Tennessee, Virginia.

[19]W. Lloyd Warner, *Yankee City* (New Haven, 1963), p. 36.

[20]*Ibid.*, p. 46.

[21](New York, 1956), pp. 95-213.

[22](New York, 1947), pp. 312-315, 325-329.

[23]Mott, *op. cit.*, p. 303. [24]*Ibid.*, p. 315.

[25]Letter from Henriette Gelber, William Morrow and Company, Inc., Dec. 13, 1967. Morrow was the original publisher of the Perry Mason books. I have had to generalize on the sales patterns of mysteries from her sales figures for these, from the fact that mysteries did not make the annual best seller list when they were issued and from the fact that Pocket Books began in 1939. Mysteries by other authors appear to have sold more widely during the 1930's. Although none of the publishers of mysteries except Morrow would release detailed sales figures, there is enough discussion of mysteries in print during the 1930's to indicate that by then they had a fairly wide audience.

[26]Letter from Alma Triner, Director of Public Relations, Crowell Collier and MacMillan, Inc., January 8, 1968. I am most grateful to Morrow and Crowell Collier and MacMillan for providing me with these detailed figures. Pocket Books was also extremely helpful. Most publishers, for one reason or another, declined to issue any greater details than total sales in their own edition or in all editions and many refused to do even this.

[27]There are no books for 1917.

CHAPTER 2

[1]The year 1910 marks the last census in which the country's rural population exceeded its urban population. An urban area is defined as having 2500 or more residents. *Historical Statistics of the United States*, p. 14.

[2]George Kennan, *American Diplomacy, 1900-1950* (Chicago, 1951), p. 5.

[3]Norman, Oklahoma, 1966.

[4]Milne, *The American Political Novel*, p. 65.

[5](New York, 1951), p. xi.

[6]Vernon Parrington, *Main Currents of American Thought* (New York, 1927), Vol. III, p. xxviii.

[7]Gunnar Myrdal, *An American Dilemma* (New York, 1966), p. 8.

[8]Tarkington, *Penrod*, p. 215. [9]p. 151

[10]p. 445.

[11]Handlin, *Race and Nationality in American Life* (Garden City, 1957), p. 138.

[12]John Higham, *Strangers in the Land* (New York, 1955), pp. 177-178.

[13]Handlin, *Race and Nationality in American Life*, p. 82 ff. The study was done comparing new immigrants with the descendants of earlier immigrants, biasing the results in favor of those who had grown up and been educated in America.

[14]Tarkington, p. 257.

[15]*Race and Nationality in American Life*, p. 52.

[16]In *The Eyes of the World*.

[17]George H. Soulé, *Prosperity Decade* 1917-1929 (London, 1947), p. 65.

[18]p. 346. [19]*The Eyes of the World*, p. 460.

[20]Kenneth Lynn, *The Dream of Success* (Boston, 1955), p. 7.

[21]*When A Man's A Man*, p. 84. [22]*Ibid.*, p. 118.

[23]New York, Knopf, 1964. [24]*The American Mind*, p. 419.

[25]Considered the basis of American values in David Potter, *People of Plenty* (Chicago, 1955).

[26]Allen, "Best Sellers, 1900-1935," p. 4.

[27]A study of the courtship and kinship relations in the best sellers of 1907 to 1916 and 1940 to 1949 is the major part of an unpublished Ph.D. dissertation by Anna Lee Hopson, *Best Sellers: Media of Mass Expression*, Radcliffe College and Harvard University, December, 1951.

[28]*When A Man's A Man*, p. 85. [29]"*K*," pp. 198-199.

[30]*Just David*, p. 98. [31]*When A Man's A Man*, p. 11.

[32]*Of Human Bondage*, p. 506. [33]*Ibid.*, pp. 658-659.

[34]*Manifest Destiny* (Baltimore, 1935), pp. 469-470.

CHAPTER 3

[1]Loos, *Gentlemen Prefer Blondes*, p. 192.

[2]B. Ibanez, *The Four Horsemen of the Apocalypse*, p. 65.

[3]H. F. May, *The End of American Innocence* (Chicago, 1964), p. 394.

[4]O. Handlin, *Race and Nationality in American Life*, p. 138.

[5]Lewis, *Babbitt*, p. 120.

[6]Loos, *Gentlemen Prefer Blondes*, pp. 28-29.

[7]Chamberlain, *Farewell to Reform* (New York, 1932), p. 305.

[8]F. L. Allen, *Only Yesterday* (New York, 1946), pp. 353-354.

[9]S. Lewis, *Main Street*, p. 257. [10]T. Smith, *Topper*, p. 241.

[11]W. Deeping, *Sorrell and Son*, p. 106.

[12]*Ibid.*, p. 107. [13]*Ibid.*, p. 366.

[14]F. L. Allen, "Best-Sellers 1900-1935," p. 20.

[15]F. Sutton, S. Harris, C. Kaysen, J. Tobin, *The American Business Creed* (Cambridge, Mass., 1956), p. 11.

[16]E. Hough, *The Covered Wagon,* p. 128.
[17]E. Wharton, *The Age of Innocence,* p. 41.
[18]A. D. Sedgwick, *The Little French Girl,* p. 211.
[19]J. Erskine, *The Private Life of Helen of Troy,* p. 71.
[20]*Ibid.,* p. 71 [21]*Ibid.,* p. 137.
[22]Lewis, *Elmer Gantry,* p. 178.
[23]E. Wharton, *The Age of Innocence,* p. 350.
[24]A. Sedgwick, *The Little French Girl,* p. 301.
[25]W. Deeping, *Sorrell and Son,* p. 210.
[26]R. Sabatini, *The Sea Hawk,* p. 96.
[27]A. Loos, *Gentlemen Prefer Blondes,* p. 151.
[28]S. Lewis, *Babbitt,* p. 170.
[29]V. Ibanez, *The Four Horsemen of the Apocalypse,* p. 159.
[30]W. Deeping, *Sorrell and Son,* p. 389.
[31]Malcolm Cowley, *The Literary Situation* (New York, 1954), p. 37.

CHAPTER 4

[1]Kenneth Roberts, *Northwest Passage,* p. 656.
[2]Edna Ferber, *Cimarron,* p. 216. [3]Vina Delmar, *Bad Girl,* p. 176.
[4]James Hilton, *Lost Horizon,* p. 83.
[5]Richard Hofstadter, *The Age of Reform* (New York, 1955), p. 11.
[6]Walter Edmonds, *Drums Along the Mohawk,* p. ix.
[7]Vernon Parrington, *Main Currents of American Thought,* Vol. III, p. xxviii.
[8]Daniel Boorstin, *The Genius of American Politics* (Chicago, 1953), p. 8.
[9]Vina Delmar, *Bad Girl,* p. 162.
[10]Max Brand, *Destry Rides Again,* p. 58. [11]*Ibid.,* p. 59.
[12]Walter Edmonds, *Drums Along the Mohawk,* p. 58.
[13]Kenneth Roberts, *Northwest Passage,* p. 119.
[14]Vina Delmar, *Bad Girl,* p. 184.
[15]Kenneth Roberts, *Northwest Passage,* p. 586.
[16]Hervey Allen, *Anthony Adverse,* p. 900.
[17]Gunnar Myrdal, *An American Dilemma,* p. 4.
[18]Erskine Caldwell, *God's Little Acre,* pp. 132-133.
[19]James Hilton, *Lost Horizon,* p. 68.
[20]Henry Steele Commager, *The American Mind,* p. 419.
[21]Hervey Allen, *Anthony Adverse,* p. 28.
[22]Erskine Caldwell, *God's Little Acre,* pp. 180-181.
[23]*Ibid.,* pp. 162-163.
[24]*Ibid.,* p. 163.

[25]James Hilton, *Lost Horizon,* p. 29.
[26]*Ibid.,* p. 116.

CHAPTER 5

[1]These books each sold more copies in Pocket Books than any other of the mysteries and also more than most of the non-mystery best sellers. Figures obtained from Miss Mina Ross, Director, Contract Dept., Pocket Books, Inc., letter to the author, December 28, 1967.

[2]E. S. Gardner, *The Case of the Substitute Face,* p. 71.

[3]He was writing specifically of Mickey Spillane's detective, Mike Hammer, in books which became best sellers after 1945, but the concept can be generalized. Christopher La Farge, "Mickey Spillane and His Bloody Hammer," *The Saturday Review,* November 6, 1954, pp. 11-12, 54-59, reprinted in Bernard Rosenberg and David Manning White, editors, *Mass Culture, The Popular Arts in America*, p. 178.

[4]Charles J. Rolo, "Simenon and Spillane: The Metaphysics of Murder for the Millions," *New World Writing,* No. 1 (1952), pp. 234-245. Reprinted in Rosenberg and White, *Mass Culture, The Popular Arts in America,* pp. 169-170.

[5]Hortense Powdermaker, "Hollywood and the U.S.A." from *Hollywood, The Dream Factory* (1951), reprinted in Rosenberg and White, p. 288.

[6]A. Kazin, *On Native Grounds* (New York, 1942), p. 367.

[7]Leo Gurko, *Heroes, Highbrows and the Popular Mind* (Indianapolis, 1953), pp. 184-188.

[8]E. S. Gardner, *The Case of the Substitute Face,* p. 1.

[9]Books that are spy stories rather than primarily murders are not included in this category. Ambler's mixture of the two is included and deals with the international settings largely in terms of how they affect the individual characters on a day to day basis.

[10]R. Stout, *The Rubber Band,* p. 202.
[11]S. S. Van Dine, *The Canary Murder Case,* p. 117.
[12]L. Charteris, *The Happy Highwayman,* p. 91.
[13]E. C. Bentley, *Trent's Last Case,* p. 229.
[14]Ellery Queen, *The French Powder Mystery,* p. 28.
[15]M. Page, *Fast Company,* p. 124.
[16]E. Queen, *The Egyptian Cross Mystery,* p. 133.
[17]S. S. Van Dine, *The Bishop Murder Case,* p. 5.
[18]D. Biggers, *The Chinese Parrot,* p. 151.
[19]O. Handlin, *Race and Nationality in American Life,* p. 141.
[20]S. S. Van Dine, *The Canary Murder Case,* p. 132.
[21]E. S. Gardner, *The Case of the Lame Canary,* pp. 151-152.
[22]Ellery Queen, *The Chinese Orange Mystery,* p. 298.
[23]Eric Ambler, *Journey Into Fear,* p. 6.
[24]E. S. Gardner, *The Case of the Sulky Girl,* p. 102.

[25]M. Page, *Fast Company*, p. 242.
[26]E. Ambler, *A Coffin for Dimitrios*, p. 267.
[27]S. S. Van Dine, *The Canary Murder Case*, p. 263.

CHAPTER 6

[1]Reference is to Henry May, *The End of American Innocence 1912-1917*.
[2]J. Steinbeck, *The Moon is Down*, pp. 185-186.
[3]*Ibid.*, p. 102.
[4]W. Saroyan, *The Human Comedy*, p. 120.
[5]J. Hersey, *A Bell for Adano*, p. v.
[6]*Ibid.*, p. 265.
[7]L. Douglas, *The Robe*, pp. 19-20.
[8]S. Shellabarger, *Captain From Castile*, p. 10.
[9]J. Steinbeck, *The Grapes of Wrath*, pp. 196-197.
[10]T. Costain, *The Black Rose*, p. 223.
[11]J. Struther, *Mrs. Miniver*, p. 286.
[12]T. Costain, *The Black Rose*, p. 18.
[13]*Ibid.*, p. 114.
[14]J. Marquand, *So Little Time*, p. 390.
[15]C. Morley, *Kitty Foyle*, p. 280.
[16]J. Hersey, *A Bell for Adano*, p. vi.
[17]C. Morley, *Kitty Foyle*, p. 18.
[18]L. Smith, *Strange Fruit*, p. 75.
[19]J. Marquand, *So Little Time*, p. 104.
[20]W. Saroyan, *The Human Comedy*, p. 146.
[21]E. Hemingway, *For Whom the Bell Tolls*, p. 16.
[22]R. Marshall, *Kitty*, p. 87.
[23]J. Steinbeck, *The Grapes of Wrath*, pp. 101-102.
[24]E. Knight, *Lassie-Come-Home*, p. 7.
[25]B. Williams, *Leave Her to Heaven*, p. 200.
[26]A. Langley, *A Lion Is In the Streets*, p. 25.
[27]R. Marshall, *Kitty*, p. 147.
[28]J. Steinbeck, *The Grapes of Wrath*, pp. 19-20.
[29]*Ibid.*, p. 378.
[30]S. Maugham, *The Razor's Edge*, p. 121.
[31]M. Rawlings, *The Yearling*, p. 21.
[32]J. Struther, *Mrs. Miniver*, p. 4.
[33]H. MacInnes, *Above Suspicion*, p. 33.
[34]J. Marquand, *So Little Time*, p. 271.
[35]J. Hersey, *A Bell for Adano*, p. v.
[36]A. Langley, *A Lion Is In the Streets*, p. 99.
[37]F. Werfel, *The Song of Bernadette*, p. 549.
[38]J. Marquand, *So Little Time*, p. 595.

[39] A. J. Cronin, *The Green Years*, p. 247.
[40] *Ibid.*, p. 347.
[41] E. Goudge, *Green Dolphin Street*, pp. 398-399.
[42] M. Rawlings, *The Yearling*, pp. 323-324.
[43] S. Maugham, *The Razor's Edge*, p. 228.
[44] E. Vance, *Escape*, p. 224.
[45] J. Steinbeck, *The Grapes of Wrath*, p. 20.
[46] J. Hilton, *So Well Remembered*, p. 189.
[47] E. Hemingway, *For Whom the Bell Tolls*, p. 41.
[48] J. Steinbeck, *The Grapes of Wrath*, p. 127.

BIBLIOGRAPHY

This is a list of supplemental material that was consulted in addition to the best selling novels. Valuable additions to the printed material were letters from representatives of The Book-of-the-Month Club, The Literary Guild, and numerous publishing houses. Publishers who allowed the release of the most valuable information were Crowell, Collier and MacMillan, William Morrow and Company, and Pocket Books. To these I am greatly indebted.

The list that follows enumerates books, articles, and unpublished scholarly material which provided valuable background information and analytical material for this study.

Aaron, Daniel. *Men of Good Hope.* New York: Oxford University Press, 1961.

Allen, Frederick Lewis. "Best-Sellers: 1900-1935," *Saturday Review of Literature*, Vol. XIII, No. 6, December 7, 1935, pp. 3-4, 20-26.

———. *Only Yesterday.* New York: Bantam Books, 1946.

Banker, Robert. "What Makes a Book Sell?" *Publishers Weekly*, Vol. 166, No. 23, December 4, 1954, pp. 2179-2182.

Book-of-the-Month Club. *The First 40 Years of the Book-of-the-Month Club.* New York, 1966.

———. *Interesting Facts About the Book-of-the-Month Club and its Role in American Literary History.* New York, 1967.

Boorstin, Daniel. *The Genius of American Politics.* Chicago: University of Chicago Press, 1953.

Chamberlain, John. *Farewell to Reform.* Chicago: Quadrangle Paperbacks, 1965.

Commager, Henry Steele. *The American Mind.* New Haven: Yale University Press, 1950.

Cowley, Malcolm. *The Literary Situation.* New York: The Viking Press, 1954.

Curti, Merle E. *The Growth of American Thought.* New York: Harper and Brothers, 1943.

Galbraith, John Kenneth. *American Capitalism: The Concept of Countervailing Power.* Boston: Houghton Mifflin Co., 1952.

Gurko, Leo. *Heroes, Highbrows and the Popular Mind.* Indianapolis: The Bobbs-Merrill Co., 1953.

Hacker, Louis M. *The Triumph of American Capitalism.* New York: Simon and Schuster, 1940.

Hackett, Alice Payne. *60 Years of Best Sellers 1895-1955.* New York: R. R. Bowker Co., 1956.

Handlin, Oscar. *Race and Nationality in American Life.* Garden City, N. Y.: Doubleday Anchor Books, 1957.

Hansen, Marcus Lee. *The Immigrant in American History.* New York: Harper Torchbooks, 1964.

Hart, Irving Harlow. "The One Hundred Leading Authors of Best Sellers in Fiction From 1895 to 1944," *Publishers Weekly*, Vol. 149, No. 3, January 19, 1946, pp. 285-290.

Hart, James D. *The Popular Book: A History of America's Literary Taste.* New York: Oxford University Press, 1950.

Hartz, Louis. *The Liberal Tradition in America.* New York: Harcourt, Brace and Company, 1955.

Higham, John. *History.* Englewood Cliffs, N. J.: Prentice Hall, 1965.

———. *Strangers in the Land.* New York: Atheneum, 1968.

Hofstadter, Richard. *The Age of Reform.* New York: Vintage Books, 1955.

———. *Anti-Intellectualism in American Life.* New York: Alfred A. Knopf, 1964.

———. *Social Darwinism in American Thought.* Philadelphia: University of Pennsylvania Press, 1944.

Hopson, Anna Lee. *Best-Sellers: Media of Mass Expression.* Radcliffe College, unpublished Ph.D. dissertation, December 1951.

Hutchens, John K. "For Better or Worse, The Book Clubs," *New*

York Times Book Review, March 31, 1946, pp. 1, 24.

Kazin, Alfred. *On Native Grounds.* New York: Reynal and Hitchcock, 1942.

Kennan, George. *American Diplomacy 1900-1950.* New York: Mentor Books, 1961.

Kolko, Gabriel. *Wealth and Power in America.* New York: Frederick A. Praeger, 1962.

Lubell, Samuel. *The Future of American Politics.* Garden City, N. Y.: Doubleday Anchor Books, 1951.

Lynd, Robert S. & Helen Lynd. *Middletown: A Study in American Culture.* New York: Harcourt, Brace and Co., 1929.

______. *Middletown in Transition.* New York: Harcourt, Brace and Co., 1937.

Lynn, Kenneth S. *The Dream of Success.* Boston: Little, Brown and Co., 1955.

May, Henry F. *The End of American Innocence.* Chicago: Quadrangle Books, 1964.

Milne, Gordon. *The American Political Novel.* Norman, Okla.: University of Oklahoma Press, 1966.

Mott, Frank Luther. *Golden Multitudes.* New York: The MacMillan Co., 1947.

Myrdal, Gunnar. *An American Dilemma.* New York: McGraw Hill Paperbacks, 1964.

Parrington, Vernon L. *Main Currents of American Thought.* New York: Harcourt, Brace and Co., 1927.

Potter, David. *People of Plenty.* Chicago: University of Chicago Press, 1954.

Readers' Guide to Periodical Literature. New York: H. W. Wilson Co. Vol. 3-14, 1910-1945

Rosenberg, Bernard and David Manning White, eds. *Mass Culture: The Popular Arts in America.* Glencoe, Ill.: The Free Press, 1957.

This includes studies by B. Berelson, A. Dutscher, H. Gerth, I. Howe, P. Johns-Heine, S. Kracaver, C. LaFarge, P. Lazarsfeld, N. Leites, R. Merton, H. Powdermaker, C. Rolo, P. Salter, and M. Wolfenstein. Individual articles are cited in footnotes.

Soule, George H. *Prosperity Decade 1917-1929.* London: The Pilot Press, Ltd., 1947.

Stevens, George. *Lincoln's Doctor's Dog.* Philadelphia: J. B. Lippincott Co., 1938.

Sutton, Francis X., Seymour E. Harris, Carl Kaysen, James Tobin. *The American Business Creed.* Cambridge: Harvard University Press, 1956.

Tocqueville, Alexis de. *Democracy in America.* New York: Alfred A. Knopf, 1945.

United States Bureau of the Census. *Historical Statistics of the United States.* Washington, D. C.: Government Printing Office, 1960.

Waples, Douglas. Research Memorandum on Social Aspects of Reading in the Depression. Social Science Research Council, Bulletin #37, New York, 1937.

Warner, W. Lloyd. *Yankee City.* New Haven: Yale University Press, 1963.

Weeks, Edward. "What Makes a Book a Best Seller?" *New York Times Book Review,* December 20, 1935, pp. 2, 15.

Weinberg, Albert K. *Manifest Destiny.* Baltimore: The Johns Hopkins Press, 1935.

White, Morton. *Social Thought in America.* Boston: Beacon Press, 1957.

Wilson, Louis R. *The Geography of Reading.* Chicago: University of Chicago Press, 1938.

INDEX